# SPORTS HEROES AND LEGENDS™

# Roberto Clemente

Read all of the books in this exciting, action-packed biography series!

*Hank Aaron*

*Muhammad Ali*

*Lance Armstrong*

*Barry Bonds*

*Roberto Clemente*

*Joe DiMaggio*

*Tim Duncan*

*Dale Earnhardt Jr.*

*Lou Gehrig*

*Derek Jeter*

*Sandy Koufax*

*Michelle Kwan*

*Mickey Mantle*

*Jesse Owens*

*Alexx Rodriguez*

*Wilma Rudolph*

*Ichiro Suzuki*

*Tiger Woods*

# SPORTS HEROES AND LEGENDS™

# Roberto Clemente

## by Stew Thornley

TFCB Twenty-First Century Books/Minneapolis

*To the dedicated members of the Society for American Baseball Research*

Twenty-First Century Books
A division of Lerner Publishing Group
241 First Avenue North
Minneapolis, MN 55401 U.S.A.

Website address: www.lernerbooks.com

Cover photograph:
© Focus on Sport/Getty Images

Library of Congress Cataloging-in-Publication Data

Thornley, Stew.
　Roberto Clemente / by Stew Thornley.
　　　p.　cm. — (Sports heroes and legends)
　　Includes bibliographical references and index.
　　ISBN-13: 978–0–8225–5962–7 (lib. bdg. : alk. paper)
　　ISBN-10: 0–8225–5962–5 (lib. bdg. : alk. paper)
　　　1. Clemente, Roberto, 1934–1972—Juvenile literature.　2. Baseball players—Puerto Rico—Biography—Juvenile literature.　I. Title.　II. Series.
　　GV865.C439T56 2007
　　796.357092—dc22　　　　　　　　　　　　　　　　2005032496

Manufactured in the United States of America
1 2 3 4 5 6 – JR – 12 11 10 09 08 07

# Contents

# Prologue

# A Key Hit

**R**oberto Clemente stood at the plate in game seven of the 1960 World Series. As he waited for the pitch, his muscles tensed and his head bobbed. Throughout his career, he never looked comfortable in the batter's box, often stretching his arms and back and craning his neck. Even so, the pitcher was usually even more uncomfortable when Clemente was at bat.

Born and raised in Puerto Rico, Clemente spoke almost no English when he arrived in the United States to play baseball six and a half years earlier. Black Latin American players were new to the major leagues in the early 1950s. Jackie Robinson, an African American, had broken major league baseball's color barrier in 1947, but racial inequality remained a problem in the United States. Despite these circumstances, Clemente was not about to let a language barrier—or racism—stand in his way.

Only twenty-six years old in 1960, Clemente was completing his sixth season in the major leagues. It was also his best yet. He had a .314 batting average during the regular season, only the second in which he had topped .300. Besides his many hits, Clemente walked or was hit by a pitch 41 times, meaning that he had reached base safely more than 35 percent of the time. In addition, Clemente hit 16 home runs, more than doubling his previous high. He also made the National League All-Star team for the first time. Most important, Clemente had helped his team, the Pittsburgh Pirates, win the National League pennant for the first time in thirty-three years. The Pirates were locked in a fierce struggle with the New York Yankees for the world championship.

The Yankees had been the pride of the American League for the past forty seasons. This was the New York team's twenty-fifth appearance in the World Series, and the Yankees had already won the big prize eighteen times. The New Yorkers were on the verge of winning the series again—but not if Clemente had anything to say about it.

The Pirates and Yankees had split the first six games of the World Series. Clemente had gotten at least one hit in each of those games. Here, in the seventh game that would decide the series, he had not yet been on base. He needed a hit. It was the bottom of the eighth inning, and New York had a 7–5 lead. The Pirates had runners on second and third, but there were two outs.

The Yankees' Jim Coates delivered his pitch. Clemente swung and topped the ball. It appeared to be a harmless grounder toward the first baseman. Clemente took off as hard as he could for first base.

Coates pounced off the pitcher's mound, hoping to snag the grounder. He couldn't get to it, leaving first baseman Bill "Moose" Skowron to field it. Clemente raced down the line as the runner from third headed for the plate. Skowron knew he couldn't beat the speedy Pirate to first. While the Yankees watched helplessly, Clemente zipped safely across the base.

Clemente's hit had driven in another run and kept the inning going. The Pittsburgh fans stood and cheered, their hopes still alive. The fans had barely settled back into their seats when the next batter, Hal Smith, drove a ball over the left-field wall for a three-run homer, giving the Pirates a 9–7 lead. Clemente jumped in glee—a rare show of exuberance from the normally reserved player—as he crossed the plate.

The Pirates still hadn't won, though, and in the top of the ninth, the Yankees quieted the crowd by scoring two runs to tie the game. Victory came for Pittsburgh in the bottom of the inning when Bill Mazeroski led off with another home run, this one finishing the World Series and giving the Pirates the title. While Pittsburgh fans have celebrated Mazeroski's blast ever since, the single that Clemente had hustled out was every bit as big.

# Chapter One

# Early Talent

**B**aseball has been popular on the Caribbean island of Puerto Rico for more than one hundred years. The sport was reportedly first played there in the late 1800s, at about the same time that the island became a territory of the United States. Puerto Rico has its own Olympic team, but its residents are citizens of the United States. Most Puerto Ricans speak Spanish as their first language.

Puerto Rico shares a love of baseball with many of the countries in and along the Caribbean Sea. Professional leagues—often known as the winter leagues because play took place during the winter months—formed and thrived in countries such as Venezuela, Mexico, and the Dominican Republic. Starting in 1949, the champions from the different leagues often met to determine a Caribbean champion. Cuba participated in the Caribbean Series when it had a professional league, prior to

Fidel Castro's takeover in 1959. Since then, sports in Cuba have been entirely amateur.

In addition to local players, the Caribbean leagues featured players from the United States. In those days, major league salaries were far less than the millions earned by modern players. Both major league and minor league players found that playing in the winter allowed them to have lucrative year-round careers.

Puerto Rico's name is Spanish for "rich port," which comes from its long history of exporting products, like gold, sugar, and coffee. Approximately 1,000 miles to the southeast of Florida, Puerto Rico is bounded on the north by the Atlantic Ocean and on the south by the Caribbean Sea.

Jack Cassini spent most of his U.S. career in the minor leagues and was Clemente's teammate one year. For six years, Cassini played in the winter, first in Cuba and then in Puerto Rico. With his combined summer and winter income, Cassini said, "I made more money playing there and in the States than if I had gone to the big leagues."

For many players, winter baseball was more than a way to make money. The Caribbean leagues gave players a chance to sharpen their skills, which helped them when they got back to the United States in the spring. Puerto Rico, in particular, was known as a great place for young players hoping to make it big.

Tony Oliva, who became a star hitter for the Minnesota Twins in the 1960s, played for Arecibo in the Puerto Rican League during the winter of 1963–1964. Oliva believes his time in Puerto Rico led to his success in the major leagues. Following his winter in the Puerto Rican League, Oliva went on to become the American League Rookie of the Year. Author Thomas E. Van Hyning has even called Puerto Rico "major league baseball's launching pad."

Puerto Rico has produced many great players of its own, including Pedro "Perucho" Cepeda. Because of his dark skin color, Perucho never got a chance to play in the U.S. major leagues, although his son, Orlando, did and eventually made the National Baseball Hall of Fame.

But the greatest Puerto Rican player of all was Roberto Clemente. Roberto was born on August 18, 1934, to Melchor Clemente and Luisa Walker de Clemente in Carolina, Puerto Rico. Carolina is slightly east of the Puerto Rican capital of San Juan. Roberto was the youngest of Luisa's seven children (two of whom were from a previous marriage).

Melchor was a foreman, overseeing sugarcane cutters. He also used his truck to help a construction company deliver sand and gravel to building sites. Luisa washed laundry for another family and also worked in different jobs to assist the laborers at the sugarcane plantation. The Clementes weren't rich, but they always had enough to get by.

Roberto contributed to the family income by helping his dad load the construction trucks. He also earned money by doing small errands, such as carrying milk from the country store to a neighbor's house. Roberto used his money for a bike and to buy rubber balls. He'd bounce the balls off the walls of the house so he could practice catching them. He also liked to squeeze them to strengthen his hands.

Clemente's full name is Roberto Clemente Walker. Walker was his mother's birth name, although his father's surname (last name) is the dominant surname in the Spanish culture. Growing up, Roberto was known to his family as *Momen*, a nonsensical name given to him by one of his sisters.

Early on, it was obvious that Roberto had athletic ability as well as a deep love of sports, especially baseball. He attended games in the winter and watched the star players from the U.S. mainland. One of his favorites became Monte Irvin. Irvin played for the Newark Eagles in the Negro National League in the summer and for the San Juan Senadores of the Puerto Rican League in the winter. Irvin remembers kids hanging around the stadium. "We'd give them our bags so they could take them in and get in for free," he said. Irvin didn't know Clemente was among the kids until Clemente told him years later, when both were in the major leagues. Clemente also told Irvin that he was impressed with his throwing arm. "I had the best arm in Puerto Rico," said Irvin. "He loved to see me throw. He . . . would practice and learn how to throw like I did."

Roberto began playing baseball himself. He had to be creative to come up with equipment to play with. His first bat was a tree branch, his glove was made from a coffee bean bag, and he and his friends used a ball made from rags tied together.

Roberto kept a journal, and one of the entries said, "I loved the game so much that even though our playing field was muddy and we had many trees on it, I used to play many hours every day. The fences were about 150 feet away from home plate, and I used to hit many homers. One day I hit ten home runs in a game we started about 11 A.M. and finished about 6:30 P.M."

When Roberto was fourteen years old, he joined a slow-pitch softball team sponsored by the Sello Rojo rice company.

The team was organized by Roberto Marín, a man who became very influential in Clemente's life. Marín noticed Roberto's strong throwing arm and began using him at shortstop. He eventually moved him to the outfield. Regardless of the position he played, Roberto was sensational. "His name became known for his long hits to right field, and for his sensational catches," said Marín. "Everyone had their eyes on him."

More than twenty-five members of the National Baseball Hall of Fame once played in the Puerto Rican League. The list includes Sandy Koufax, Hank Aaron, Roy Campanella, Monte Irvin, and Willie Mays.

Roberto also participated in track and field at Vizcarrondo High School in Carolina, competing in the high jump and javelin throw. His coaches thought that he might even be good enough to represent Puerto Rico in the 1952 Olympics.

The javelin throw is somewhat similar to throwing a baseball, and it probably helped develop the muscles in Roberto's arm. But Roberto claimed that throwing the javelin in high school was only part of the reason he developed a strong arm. "My mother has the same kind of an arm, even today at seventy-four," he said in a 1964 interview. "She could throw a ball from second base to home plate with something on it. I got my arm from my mother."

While in high school, Roberto decided to focus on baseball, even though it meant giving up any dreams of participating in the Olympics in track and field. He joined a strong amateur team, the Juncos Mules.

In 1952 Clemente took part in a tryout camp in Puerto Rico that was attended by Al Campanis of the Brooklyn Dodgers of the National League. Clemente impressed Campanis with his different skills, including his speed. The Dodgers didn't sign Clemente then, but Campanis kept him in mind.

Also in 1952, Clemente caught the eye of Pedrín Zorrilla, who owned the Santurce Cangrejeros, or Crabbers, of the Puerto Rican League—a professional league. The Juncos team was to play the Manatí Athenians in Manatí, where Zorrilla had a house on the beach. Roberto Marín advised Zorrilla to go to the game. Clemente impressed Zorrilla with his fielding, especially his strong throwing arm. Afterward, Zorrilla offered Clemente a contract to play with the Cangrejeros. In this way, Roberto Marín helped to arrange the contract that made Roberto Clemente a professional baseball player.

Clemente was barely eighteen years old when he joined the Cangrejeros. As a young developing player, he was brought along slowly by the team's manager, James "Buster" Clarkson. Clarkson had had an outstanding career in the Negro Leagues in the United States and played many winters in Puerto Rico. He did get the chance to play in the major leagues in 1952, but Clarkson was thirty-seven years old at the time.

Like many great black ballplayers, Clarkson's best years were behind him by the time he got his chance in the majors. Two other such players were Willard "Ese Hombre" Brown and Bob Thurman, who were top players in the Negro Leagues. Both were outfielders (with Thurman also doing some pitching) on the Santurce team that Clemente became a part of in the winter of 1952–1953.

From the 1880s until the mid-1940s, African Americans and dark-skinned Latino baseball players weren't allowed in the U.S. major leagues. Instead, they played in the U.S. Negro Leagues in the summer and the Caribbean leagues in the winter. Some of the top Negro League players, including Satchel Paige, Cool Papa Bell, and Josh Gibson, were later inducted into the National Baseball Hall of Fame.

Clemente admired Thurman and once had the chance to pinch-hit for him. He hit a double to win the game and received congratulations from Thurman. Despite the big hit, Clemente didn't play much his first winter in the Puerto Rican League.

He began playing more in the 1953–1954 season and even played in the league's All-Star Game. (The star of the All-Star Game, however, was Henry Aaron of the Caguas-Guayama Criollos, who had four hits—including two home runs—and drove in five runs. Aaron later set the record for the most career home runs in the major leagues.) By midseason, Clemente's name was appearing, along with Aaron's, in the list of the league leaders in batting average. Clemente finished the season with a .288 batting average, sixth best in the league.

Clemente credited his manager in Santurce, Buster Clarkson, with helping him as he started his professional career. "I played for his team and I was just a kid. He insisted the other players allow me to take batting practice and he helped me." Clemente also said that during batting practice Clarkson put a bat behind his left foot to help him stop dragging his foot when he hit.

The Brooklyn Dodgers had remembered Clemente from his tryout with Al Campanis. Emil "Buzzie" Bavasi, the Dodgers' vice president, said that during the 1953–1954 season he got a call from a scout of theirs in Puerto Rico saying that Clemente could be signed by the Dodgers.

Other major league teams had noticed Clemente too and were in the hunt to sign him. One of the teams was the New York Giants. The Giants and Dodgers were the two National League teams in New York (Brooklyn is a part of New York City), and the teams were great rivals. Brooklyn outbid the Giants, and Clemente agreed to sign with them. The Milwaukee Braves also made an offer, one that was reportedly much more than the Dodgers'. But Clemente stuck with his decision. He knew that New York City had a large Puerto Rican population and looked forward to playing for a team in that city. On February 19, 1954, Clemente signed a contract with the Brooklyn Dodgers.

# Chapter Two

# A Season in Montreal

Although Roberto Clemente joined the Brooklyn Dodgers organization, it didn't mean that he would play immediately in the major leagues. Most players start in the minor leagues, where they can continue to improve and work their way up to the majors.

Clemente was in a special category, however. The Dodgers had given Clemente a bonus of $10,000 when they signed him. Under rules in effect at that time, if a team signed a player for a combined bonus and salary of greater than $4,000, the team had to keep the player on its major league roster for at least two years. Otherwise the player could be selected by another team in a draft held at the end of each season.

Despite the risk of losing Clemente, the Dodgers sent him to the minor leagues in 1954. Clemente played for the Montreal Royals, one of the Dodgers' farm teams.

## FACING RACISM

Clemente experienced segregation when he began playing for the Royals. The city of Montreal was relatively free of open racism, although he reported that he was scolded by a fan for talking to a white woman outside of the Royals' stadium. One of the cities in the International League was Richmond, Virginia. Here, black players were not allowed to eat in the same restaurants or stay at the same hotels as their teammates.

Various reasons are given for why the Dodgers didn't keep Clemente at the major league level. One is that they never intended to keep Clemente. Some people suspect that the Dodgers signed him just to keep their rivals, the New York Giants, from getting him. New York already had Willie Mays, and an outfield consisting of Mays and Clemente would have made the Giants very hard to beat. By signing Clemente, the Dodgers kept him away from the competition.

Clemente's skin color is also brought up as a reason. Even though the color barrier had been broken by the Dodgers when they signed Jackie Robinson, many people believed that a type of quota system still existed. Teams may have had an informal agreement among themselves not to have too many black players at any one time. The Dodgers already had a number of African American players, so it has been claimed that they sent Clemente to the minor leagues to keep the team from going over its self-imposed limit.

Buzzie Bavasi was the person who could make the final decision on whether Clemente would play with Brooklyn in 1954 or in the minor leagues. Bavasi later said the reports were false that the Dodgers were only trying to keep Clemente from the New York Giants.

On the subject of Clemente being black, Bavasi said that although their concern "had nothing to do with quotas," race was a part of it. "The thought [among people in the Dodgers organization] was that too many minorities might be a problem with the white players," Bavasi wrote. " 'Not so,' I said. Winning was the important thing." The board of directors called in Jackie Robinson to ask his opinion of the situation.

Robinson wanted to know which player would have to leave the team if Clemente joined, and Bavasi told him it would be out-fielder George Shuba. Robinson answered that Shuba wasn't among the best players on the club, but he was the most popular. According to Bavasi, "With that he shocked me by saying, and I quote: 'If I were the GM [general manager], I would not bring Clemente to the club and send Shuba or any other white player down. If I did this, I would be setting our program back five years.'" So, with Jackie Robinson reportedly influencing the decision, Clemente remained in the minor leagues for all of 1954.

---

❝I couldn't speak English," Clemente once said, recalling his early years playing baseball in the United States and Canada. "Not to speak thc language . . . that is a terrible problem.❞

—ROBERTO CLEMENTE

---

Most accounts of Clemente's time with the Royals claim that the Dodgers were trying to "hide" Clemente in Montreal. In other words, they played him rarely, hoping that other teams wouldn't notice him and, as a result, wouldn't draft him at the end of the season.

Clemente himself later claimed that the treatment went beyond seldom playing him. "The idea was to make me look bad. If I struck out, I stayed in there. If I played well, I was benched," he said.

A game-by-game check of Montreal's 1954 season, however, doesn't back up Clemente's claim or the claims that he was being hidden. (The game-by-game analysis was done with box scores of the Montreal Royals games, published in the

**17**

*Sporting News* in 1954.) Early in the season, Clemente was in the starting lineup five games in a row. He had one hit in the first of those games and three more in the next. He continued starting and was hitless in his next three games. At that point, he came out of the starting lineup.

It's true that Clemente, after getting those five straight starts early in the year, played little over the first three months of the season with the Royals. Yet this was hardly unusual for a nineteen-year-old in his first season of organized baseball.

Montreal manager Max Macon, up to the time of his death in 1989, denied that he was under any orders to restrict Clemente's playing time to keep other teams' scouts from seeing him play. "The only orders I had were to win and draw big crowds," Macon said.

For much of the year, the Royals had a full crop of reliable outfielders in Dick Whitman, Gino Cimoli, and Jack Cassini. In addition the Dodgers sent outfielder Sandy Amoros down to Montreal early in the season. Amoros hit well enough during his time with the Royals that he was recalled to Brooklyn in July. The crowded outfield situation didn't leave a lot of playing time for a newcomer like Clemente. Very often he was used as a late-inning defensive replacement for Cassini.

When Clemente did play, he struggled with his hitting. In early July, his batting average was barely over .200. Part of that can be attributed to his infrequent playing time; it's hard for a batter to get in a groove and hit well when he doesn't play regularly. On the other hand, it's hard for a player to get regular playing time if he's not hitting well.

### Shaking Off an Injury

Clemente suffered a strange injury in a game against the Havana Sugar Kings. He was running in from his position at the end of an inning and tripped while crossing the pitcher's mound. He turned his ankle, and it was thought he would be out for a week. Lucky for Clemente, he was back in the starting lineup two nights later and had three hits—helping Montreal win the game.

Macon said the reason he didn't use Clemente much at that time was that he "swung wildly," especially at pitches that were outside the strike zone. "If you had been in Montreal that year, you wouldn't have believed how ridiculous some pitchers made him look," Macon said.

Clemente got more chances when a left-handed pitcher was on the mound for the opposing team. In general, right-handed hitters do better against left-handed pitchers and vice versa. Macon was known for platooning—that is, substituting his players in such a way as to get these favorable matchups. Clemente often split time in the lineup with Whitman, a left-handed hitter.

## GAME WINNERS

Both of Clemente's home runs with the Royals won the game on the spot. His first, on Sunday, July 25, broke a 6–6 tie in the bottom of the tenth inning. His second home run came in the second game of a doubleheader on Sunday, September 5. The game was scheduled for seven innings. (It was normal for one game of a doubleheader to be only seven innings in the minor leagues at that time.) The game went into extra innings. With the score still tied in the bottom of the eighth, Clemente homered off Lynn Lovenguth of Syracuse to end the game and win it for the Royals.

Through June and July, Clemente often went long stretches without seeing any action. Then, on July 25, he entered the first game of a doubleheader against the Havana Sugar Kings in the ninth inning. The game was tied and went into extra innings. With one out in the bottom of the tenth, Clemente came to the plate and hit a home run to win it for the Royals.

Macon rewarded him for his feat by starting him in the second game of the doubleheader. It was Clemente's first start in nearly three weeks. Through the rest of the season, Clemente started every game in which the opposition started a left-handed pitcher.

Clemente had a few more highlights during this time. Near the end of July, he came to bat in the top of the ninth inning of a scoreless game in Toronto, Canada. Clemente doubled and went on to score to put Montreal ahead. The Royals won the game, 2–0.

The next time the Royals were in Toronto, three weeks later, Clemente helped them win in a different way. Montreal had an 8–7 lead over the Maple Leafs in the bottom of the ninth. Toronto had a chance to tie the score, but Clemente threw out a runner at home plate to end the game.

Some biographers have claimed that Clemente didn't play in the Royals' final twenty-five games of the season. But that's incorrect. In fact, Clemente was playing somewhat regularly by the end of the season.

Late in August, Clemente had two triples and a single in a game at Richmond, Virginia, although the Royals still lost the game. A week later he hit a home run to win the game for Montreal and give the Royals a sweep of a doubleheader against Syracuse.

Teammate Jack Cassini said of Clemente, "You knew he was going to play in the big leagues. He had a great arm and he could run." When Clemente began playing regularly against left-handed pitchers, the Royals improved their record and rose in the standings, finishing in second place.

Clemente finished his minor league season with a batting average of .257. He played in 87 games for Montreal.

By the end of the season, it had become clear to Buzzie Bavasi and the rest of the Brooklyn Dodgers organization that other teams were interested in Clemente. A draft would be held in November. The Pittsburgh Pirates, who'd had the worst record in the majors in 1954, got the first pick, and it looked like they would draft Clemente.

Bavasi wasn't ready to give up. If he could get the Pirates to draft a different player off the Montreal Royals' roster, Clemente would remain with the Dodgers organization. (Each team could lose only one player, so if a different Montreal player were taken, then no other team could draft Clemente or any other Royals player.)

Bavasi said he went to Branch Rickey Sr., the executive vice president and general manager of the Pittsburgh Pirates. Rickey had been running the Brooklyn Dodgers before going to Pittsburgh, and he had tried to persuade Bavasi to come with him. Bavasi decided to remain in Brooklyn, but Rickey told him, "Should I need help at any time, all I had to do was pick up the phone," according to Bavasi.

Bavasi tried to use this offer of help to get Rickey to draft a different player, pitcher John Rutherford, off the Royals roster. Rickey said he would do it. Confident that they would be able to keep Clemente, Bavasi was dismayed to learn two days later that the deal was off and that the Pirates were going to draft Clemente.

## A BARGAIN FOR THE PIRATES

It cost the Pirates $4,000 to draft Clemente from the Dodgers organization, but Branch Rickey Sr. thought he was worth even more than that. "I had a good line on this boy," Rickey said. "Three different members of the scouting staff observed his play. On the reports I would have paid more than the $4,000 it cost the club. I would have paid $10,000 or even gone as high as $30,000 for him."

Dodgers owner Walter O'Malley was set on Clemente. "It seemed that Walter O'Malley and Mr. Rickey got in another argument and it seems Walter called Mr. Rickey every name in the book," explained Bavasi. "Thus, we lost Roberto."

# Chapter Three

# Breaking into the Majors

At the time he was being drafted by Pittsburgh, Clemente was in Puerto Rico, playing for the Santurce Cangrejeros and on his way to his best ever winter season. He again played with Bob Thurman, but the Santurce outfield had a new addition in 1954–1955. He was Willie Mays, who had just led the New York Giants to the World Series championship. Mays had a great season for New York and ended up being named the National League's Most Valuable Player (MVP).

An outfield of Clemente, Mays, and Thurman ranks as one of the best ever in the Puerto Rican League. By midseason, Santurce manager Herman Franks was calling Clemente "the best player in the league, except for Willie Mays."

By this time, Clemente and Mays had been providing some real highlights. In late November, the Cangrejeros were behind by one run going into the ninth inning of a game against

Caguas-Guyama. Clemente led off the ninth with a single, and Mays then hit a two-run homer to give Santurce a 7–6 win. Not long after that, the pair starred in another 7–6 win. Mays hit two home runs and Clemente one home run in an eleven-inning win over Mayaguez.

Both players homered in the league's All-Star Game on December 12, leading their North team to a 7–5 win. By this time, Mays, Clemente, and Thurman were the top three players in the league in batting average, and Santurce moved into first place.

Clemente attended school while playing baseball for Santurce in 1954. He took classes in the morning and played ball at night. He graduated from the Rio Piedras Business Institute in December 1954.

While things were going well on the baseball diamond, Clemente faced some other difficulties. In early December 1954, Clemente visited his half brother, Luis, who was in the hospital with a brain tumor. As he was leaving the hospital, a drunk driver struck Clemente's car. The accident damaged some of Clemente's spinal disks. The back injury lingered and hampered Clemente for the rest of his baseball career. Then, on New Year's Eve, Luis died.

Back on the field, Santurce finished first in the Puerto Rican League. The top three teams advanced to the playoffs, so the Cangrejeros had to win another series to capture the league title. They did, defeating Caguas-Guayama, four games to one. Clemente had four hits, including two doubles, and drove in four runs in the first game of the series, which Santurce won. Caguas-Guayama won the next game, but the Cangrejeros then won three in a row to finish the series. As champions of the Puerto Rican League, they would go on to the Caribbean Series.

The Caribbean Series took place in Caracas, Venezuela, in February 1955. In addition to Santurce, teams from Cuba, Panama, and Venezuela participated. It was a double round-robin tournament. That meant each team would play each of the other teams twice, and the team with the best record at the end would be the champion.

The Cangrejeros won their first two games and then faced Venezuela's Navegantes de Magallanes. The game went into extra innings. Clemente singled to open the bottom of the eleventh inning, and Mays followed with a home run to win the game, 4–2.

One more win would clinch at least a tie for the title for Santurce. The Cangrejeros' fourth game was a rematch against Almendares of Cuba, a team they had defeated in their first game. In this game, Almendares opened up a 5–0 lead, but

Santurce battled back to win. Clemente drove in two runs to help in the comeback effort.

Don Zimmer was Clemente's teammate in Santurce and later managed him in the Puerto Rican League. Zimmer said, "He was flamboyant—just the way he ran, like a colt. He was a complete player." Zimmer had a long career as a major league manager and coach.

Santurce played Carta Vieja of Panama with a chance to take the championship. Clemente had a triple as the Cangrejeros scored three times in the top of the first. In the third, Clemente had another triple as Santurce scored four runs to take a 7–0 lead. Santurce won the game, 11–3. The win wrapped up the championship for Santurce.

It was the second Caribbean Series title for Santurce in three years. Clemente had been a part of the team that had won the championship in 1953, but he didn't play in the series that year. This time he was a key member of the winning team. Santurce shortstop Don Zimmer, who was voted the Most Valuable Player of the Caribbean Series, said, "It might have been the best winter club ever assembled."

Soon afterward, Clemente was back in training camp with the Pittsburgh Pirates, hoping to earn a spot in the major leagues. The Pirates had been keeping an eye on Clemente over the winter. "He can run, throw, and hit. He needs much polishing, though, because he is a rough diamond," said Branch Rickey Sr.

One of the ways Clemente impressed the Pirates in his first spring training with them was with his speed. He ran the 60-yard dash in 6.6 seconds, the fastest on the team.

Rickey's son, Branch Rickey Jr. (known as "Twig"), was also an executive with the Pirates. Twig said, "I've watched the boy in Puerto Rico, and I keep trying not to believe my own thoughts about him for next year. He's got better than an outside chance to make our club."

The Pirates were loaded with outfielders when they began spring training in Florida in March 1955. Clemente would have plenty of competition for a spot on the team. After the first week of training camp, Clemente earned some good words from Pirates manager Fred Haney. "The boy has the tools, there's no doubt about that. And he takes to instruction readily. Certainly I have been pleased with what I have seen," Haney said. "He has some faults, which were expected, but let's wait and see."

Clemente's chances were helped when Frank Thomas, the Pirates' best outfielder, held out for more money and missed the first part of spring training. Thomas then got sick and missed more time. Clemente took advantage of this opportunity and made the team.

Clemente's original number with the Pirates was 13, but early in the season, he switched to 21, a number that became strongly associated with him. Clemente chose the number because his full name, Roberto Clemente Walker, has twenty-one letters in it.

Clemente didn't play in the first three regular season games. He was finally in the starting lineup, playing right field, for the first game of a doubleheader on Sunday, April 17, 1955. The Pirates were playing the Brooklyn Dodgers at Forbes Field in Pittsburgh. In his first-ever major league game, Clemente had to face the team that had let him go the year before.

Clemente came to the plate with two outs in the bottom of the first inning. He hit a ground ball toward the shortstop, Pee Wee Reese. Reese got his glove on the grounder, but he couldn't field it cleanly. Clemente had his first hit. He followed that by scoring his first run to give Pittsburgh a 1–0 lead. Unfortunately, Brooklyn came back in later innings to win the game.

Clemente started the second game of the doubleheader as well. This time he played center field. He was also the leadoff batter. Clemente had a double during the game, but the Pirates were unable to score and trailed the Dodgers, 3–0, going into the bottom of the eighth. Clemente got another hit, a single, as part of a two-run rally that closed the gap. The Pirates still lost, though.

Clemente had two triples in a game on Sunday, July 3, helping the Pirates beat the Dodgers in the first game of a doubleheader. His triple in the fourth inning led to the run that tied the game. And his triple in the fifth inning led to the winning run.

Pittsburgh's next game was in New York, against the Giants. Clemente hit an impressive inside-the-park home run, but the Pirates lost again. At this point, their won-lost record was 0–6. And Pittsburgh lost two more games before winning their first game of the season.

Clemente led the team in batting average over the first three weeks of 1955. Once on the base paths, Clemente was even more exciting. "When he starts moving around the bases he draws the 'Ohs' and 'Ahs' of the folks in the ballpark," wrote

31

Jack Hernon in the *Sporting News*. Hernon added, "The fleet Puerto Rican was a stickout on defense."

Forbes Field, the home of the Pirates, was a classic ballpark that had opened in 1909. The outfield fence was a brick wall. It was only 300 feet from home plate to the wall down the right-field line. But the wall jutted out and changed directions. Clemente learned the angles and how to play balls that bounced off the fence. He could corral long hits quickly and, with his great arm, opposing base runners were careful about trying to take an extra base.

Less than a third of the way through the season, Clemente already had 10 assists, and he also made some outstanding catches. "The Pittsburgh fans have fallen in love with his spectacular fielding and his deadly right arm," wrote Les Biederman, a reporter who covered the Pirates.

During his rookie season, Clemente's roommate was another Latino player, Cuban Roman Mejias. When the Pirates were in New York, Clemente and Mejias liked to dine at a Puerto Rican restaurant near the team's hotel. Their favorite foods were beans, rice, steaks, and fried bananas.

Clemente's rambunctious style in the field could be costly, though. In May he made a nice catch in St. Louis, but he ran into the wall and hurt his finger. The injury caused him to miss a few games.

Clemente slowed down in his hitting as the season went along, in part because he still had trouble laying off pitches that were out of the strike zone. However, he became known as a good "bad-ball hitter," able to make good contact on bad pitches. Jack Cassini had played in the minors with Clemente the year before and was impressed with Clemente's talent at the plate.

---

❝ *He could hit. He didn't need a strike. The best way to pitch him was right down the middle of the plate.* ❞

—JACK CASSINI

---

The Pirates went on to finish in last place in the National League for the fourth year in a row. But Branch Rickey Sr. still believed that young players such as Clemente could help turn the team around in future seasons.

Clemente played 124 games for the Pirates in 1955 and had a batting average of .255. He walked only 18 times. Drawing bases on balls (walks) wasn't a strong spot for him, nor would it ever really become one. Most of the time he reached base, it was by a hit. While it wasn't a sensational rookie season, Clemente had earned a regular spot in the Pirates' outfield. More than that, his exciting style of play made the fans look forward to seeing more of him.

# Chapter Four

# Moving On Up

F ollowing his rookie season in the major leagues, Clemente returned to Puerto Rico in the fall of 1955. Reports suggested that he might not play winter ball in his homeland and instead would begin college and study engineering. Clemente ended up back on the diamond, however, playing another season for Santurce, which won the regular season pennant but was knocked out of the playoffs by Caguas-Guayama.

Back on the mainland in 1956, Clemente had a new boss in Pittsburgh. Bobby Bragan had taken over as manager from Fred Haney. Bragan was well liked by the players although he was also strict. In the second game of the season, Clemente missed a signal for a bunt. Bragan fined Clemente for the mistake. He also fined another player, Dale Long. Biographer Kal Wagenheim suggested that the fines fired the players up since both Long and Clemente started hitting well soon after.

## An Outstanding Outfield

Early in the 1956 season, the Pirates traded to get outfielder Bill Virdon from the St. Louis Cardinals. To make sure that Clemente would have a regular spot in the outfield, manager Bobby Bragan moved Frank Thomas from the outfield to third base. The Pittsburgh outfield of Clemente, Virdon, and Lee Walls was regarded as the best in the league defensively.

The Pirates were in first place in mid-June, but an eight-game losing streak dropped them to fifth place and ended their pennant hopes. Even so, they avoided last place for the first time since 1951, and they were showcasing one of the major league's most exciting players.

In the outfield, Clemente had 17 assists, a sign of his strong throwing arm. At the plate, he had a batting average of .311, third best in the National League. In the late 1950s and early 1960s, pitchers dominated baseball. Batters had a much tougher time breaking .300 than baseball players in the 1980s, 1990s, and 2000s.

Two of Clemente's biggest hits were game-winning home runs in July. On Saturday, July 21, the Pirates trailed the Reds, 3–1, in the top of the ninth but had two runners on base as

Clemente came to the plate. The Cincinnati pitcher was Brooks Lawrence, who had already won 13 games that season and hadn't yet lost a game. Clemente changed that, hitting a three-run homer, giving the Pirates a 4–3 win, and spoiling Lawrence's perfect record.

The following Wednesday, the Pirates were at home, playing the Chicago Cubs. Chicago led, 8–5, but Pittsburgh loaded the bases with no outs. Clemente was due up, and the Cubs brought in a new pitcher, Jim Brosnan. On Brosnan's first pitch, Clemente hit a long drive to left-center field. Hank Foiles, Bill Virdon, and Dick Cole raced around the bases toward home plate with the runs that would tie the game. Clemente also tore around the diamond.

Manager Bobby Bragan was coaching at third base and held up his arms, giving Clemente the signal to stop at third. With no one out and good hitters coming up, Bragan figured they'd still get Clemente home with the winning run. He didn't want to take a chance on Clemente being thrown out at the plate on this play. Clemente, however, ignored his manager, kept running, and was safe at home. The inside-the-park grand-slam home run won the game for the Pirates.

Bragan wasn't happy about Clemente deliberately disobeying the sign he gave. But since Clemente did win the game, Bragan decided not to fine him this time.

Clemente's hits were the usual way for him to reach base because he rarely walked. He drew only 13 bases on balls in 1956, and at one point during the season he went 50 games without walking. Branch Rickey Sr. wasn't concerned, though. "His value is in not taking bases on balls because he can hit the bad pitches," said Rickey. "If I tried to teach him to wait for a good pitch, I'd simply make a bad hitter out of him. The cure would be worse than the disease. He'll cure his own ailments simply by experience."

In a list published by the *Sporting News*, Clemente was ranked as one of the fastest players in baseball in 1956. He was timed at getting from the batter's box to first base in 3.6 seconds.

Clemente went to Puerto Rico during the break for the All-Star Game in July, and at the end of the 1956 season, he headed home again to play another season for Santurce. A couple of significant events took place between Christmas and New Year's Day. First, Santurce owner Pedrín Zorrilla sold the team. A few days later, the new owner of the Cangrejeros traded several players, including Clemente, to Caguas-Rio Piedras.

Although he may have been disappointed by being traded, Clemente kept it to himself. Others on the team, however, were outraged. Manager Monchile Concepción resigned, and pitcher Rubén Gómez, after learning of the trade, refused to put on his uniform for Santurce's next game and left the stadium where the Cangrejeros were to play.

---

### FOILED BY A FRIEND

The pitcher who stopped Clemente's hitting streak in the winter of 1956–1957, Luis "Tite" Arroyo, had taken Clemente to the mainland for his first spring-training trip in 1954. At the request of Santurce owner Pedrín Zorrilla, Arroyo flew to Miami with Clemente, then took him on a bus to training camp and got him checked into a hotel. In 1956 and 1957, Clemente and Arroyo were teammates on the Pittsburgh Pirates.

---

Clemente was leading the league in batting average and had gotten at least one hit in 18 consecutive games when he was traded. He continued his hitting streak, which reached 23 to set a new Puerto Rican League record. His streak was snapped when he was held hitless in a game by Luis "Tite" Arroyo, a longtime friend and teammate on the Pirates who was pitching for the San Juan Senadores in the winter. Clemente finished the winter with a batting average of .396.

---

*❝[Clemente is] a shining star to many, many people. He grows and grows over time. . . . The sad part is that there are not enough TV pictures of him. He made so many great plays that people can only talk about. You could never capture the magnificence of the man.❞*

—JOE L. BROWN, PIRATES GENERAL MANAGER

---

Clemente's batting eye was certainly sharp. His back continued to bother him, though, and he reported a day late to spring training in 1957 as a result. Bobby Bragan made light of the backache because Clemente had always played well even when he complained of aches and pains. "The case history of Clemente is the worse he feels, the better he plays," reported the *Sporting News*, which quoted Bragan as saying, "I'd rather have a Clemente with some ailment than a Clemente who says he feels great with no aches or pains."

Clemente's ability to play through pain and perform well may have contributed toward charges that he wasn't really hurt. This time, however, the back problems forced him to miss the first two games of the 1957 regular season. In all,

Clemente played in only 111 games for Pittsburgh in 1957 (36 fewer than in 1956), and his batting average dropped to .253. The back problems lingered into the winter, and Clemente wasn't able to play in the Puerto Rican League until mid-January of 1958.

The Pirates had finished tied for last place with the Chicago Cubs in 1957, but they made a big jump in 1958. Danny Murtaugh, who joined the team in the middle of the previous season, managed them. Clemente was feeling better physically, and he helped his team get off to a good start in the opening game. He had three hits, one of which tied the game in the eighth inning, against Milwaukee. The Pirates eventually won the game in fourteen innings.

---

❝*I never once think about the Pittsburgh Pirates without thinking of Roberto Clemente.*❞

STEVE BLASS, CLEMENTE'S TEAMMATE

---

Clemente continued to hit well. He had three hits again in a 4–3 win in Cincinnati on April 25. One was a single in the sixth inning when the Pirates were trailing, 1–0. Clemente eventually scored to tie the game. The next inning he broke the tie by hitting a three-run homer.

Another game-winning home run came in Milwaukee on August 4. Clemente broke a 3–3 tie with two out in the top of the ninth with a home run off fellow Puerto Rican Juan "Terín" Pizarro (who had also been a winter teammate of Clemente's in Puerto Rico). A little over a month later, Clemente had an even more spectacular game, even though he didn't hit any homers. Instead he had three triples, which tied a National League record, in a 4–1 win over Cincinnati on September 8.

Clemente had a .289 batting average in 1958. From right field, he continued to terrorize opposing base runners, often throwing them out as they tried to take an extra base. He finished the year with 22 assists. Fans loved it when a ball was hit his way with runners on base, rising in anticipation of seeing him uncork a strong throw.

Led by Clemente, the Pirates improved greatly. After a last-place finish in 1957, Pittsburgh climbed all the way to second place, finishing only behind the Milwaukee Braves.

Clemente didn't play winter baseball in Puerto Rico in 1958–1959. He wore a different uniform—that of the United States Marine Corps Reserves. He fulfilled a six-month military commitment at Parris Island, South Carolina, and Camp LeJeune, North Carolina. The rigorous training program helped Clemente physically. He added strength by gaining ten pounds and said that his back troubles had disappeared.

During his training at the Marine Corps Recruit Depot in Parris Island, South Carolina, Clemente was promoted to private first class. He was one of only seven members out of his 130-member platoon to be promoted.

Unfortunately, Clemente had a new problem when he finally reported to the Pirates in the spring of 1959. He complained of a sore right elbow—his right arm was his throwing arm. In May he made it worse when he hit the ground hard while making a diving catch. A few nights later, he had to be taken out of a game because he couldn't throw overhanded. He missed more than a month of the season and, even after he returned to the lineup, he continued to feel pain in the elbow.

Clemente hit four home runs in 1959. Two of those homers came on the same day, and one was memorable for how far it traveled. On May 17, Clemente homered in both games of a doubleheader at Wrigley Field in Chicago. Clemente's homer in the second game, to left-center field, was estimated at 500 feet. Retired ballplayer Rogers Hornsby, one of the greatest hitters ever, said it was one of the longest home runs he had ever seen.

## ROGERS HORNSBY

Rogers Hornsby grew up in the small town of Winters, Texas, and began playing with the St. Louis Cardinals in 1915. He finished the 1924 season with a .424 batting average—the highest batting average for a professional baseball player in the twentieth century. The following year, he managed the Cardinals, as well as playing on the team. Later in his career, Hornsby played for—and sometimes managed—the New York Giants, the Boston Braves, the Chicago Cubs, and the St. Louis Browns.

Clemente played in only 105 games in 1959, and the Pirates dropped to fourth place. Clemente's batting average was .296—his highest since 1956—and he had 50 RBIs. But he and the Pirates were primed for better things in 1960.

# Chapter | Five

# A Championship Season

For the first time in several winters, Clemente played a full season in the Puerto Rican League in 1959–1960. He was on another new team, having been traded to the San Juan Senadores, and he had a batting average of .330 for them. Clemente and the Pirates hoped that he was ready for a big season back in Pittsburgh.

Another encouraging sign was that he was free of injuries. "This is the first time I ever went into a season without aches or pains," he told a reporter. "One year it was a bad back. Another year I hurt my hand. This spring I came to camp healthy."

Feeling good and tuned up from his winter play, Clemente got off to a great start in 1960. In the Pirates' second game, at home against the Reds, Clemente went three for three (three hits in three at bats) and drove in five runs as Pittsburgh won, 13–0. By the end of April, Clemente had a batting average of

.386. In just 14 games, he had scored 12 runs, drove in 14, and hit 3 home runs.

But he was just warming up. In Cincinnati, he had a home run and four RBIs on the first day of May. The 13–2 win for Pittsburgh was its ninth straight, and the team was in first place.

---

❝He's a four-letter man. He can hit, run, field, and throw. You won't find many with all of those qualifications. Some have two or three, but not many have all four.❞

—PIE TRAYNOR, PIRATES THIRD BASEMAN

---

The Pirates cooled off a bit as the season went on, but Clemente stayed hot. In May, Clemente had 25 RBIs in 27 games, raising his season total to 39. He helped Pittsburgh regain the top spot in the National League standings. For his outstanding play, the *Sporting News* named Clemente the league's Player of the Month.

The San Francisco Giants (who had moved from New York after the 1957 season), with Willie Mays, stayed close to the Pirates through the first half of June, but Pittsburgh swept a three-game series from the Giants in San Francisco. The Giants fell back, but then the Milwaukee Braves, with slugger Hank Aaron, challenged the Pirates.

In July Clemente played for the National League in the All-Star Game for the first time. He was selected as a reserve player by Walter Alston, manager of the National League team. During this time, two All-Star Games were being played each year, and Clemente appeared in both, replacing Hank Aaron in right field each time.

Following the All-Star Games, Milwaukee briefly took over first place from the Pirates. But the very next day, Clemente hit a home run and helped the Pirates to win their game and move back into first place.

On the first Friday night in August, the Pirates were locked in a scoreless battle with the Giants at Forbes Field. Wilmer "Vinegar Bend" Mizell was pitching for Pittsburgh and getting great help from his outfielders. Bill Virdon made a couple of good catches. Then Willie Mays led off the seventh inning for San Francisco with a long drive to right. Clemente chased the fly, reached out, and caught it, robbing Mays of an extra-base hit. But immediately after making the catch, Clemente crashed into the outfield wall. He hurt his knee and also ended up with a gash in his chin that needed five stitches to close up.

Clemente stayed in the game the rest of the inning, but he was replaced by Gino Cimoli (his minor league teammate in Montreal) to start the eighth. Pittsburgh eventually won the game, 1–0, which started a four-game sweep of the Giants.

47

Because of his injuries, Clemente missed the rest of the series as well as another three games.

Soon after Clemente was back on the field, he had a big game against the St. Louis Cardinals. St. Louis had beaten the Pirates the previous two nights, and the Cardinals were in second place, only three games behind Pittsburgh. In the next game, on Saturday afternoon, the Cardinals took the lead again with a run in the top of the first inning. In the bottom of the first, Pittsburgh tied the game when Clemente singled home Dick Groat. With the score still tied, Groat opened the third inning with a double, and Clemente followed with a homer. Clemente had another run-scoring single in the fourth, and Pittsburgh won the game, 4–1. Clemente had batted in all four of his team's runs.

The Pirates swept a doubleheader from the Cardinals the next day to open up a big lead in the standings. No one came close to them the rest of the season. Except for one day, the Pirates had been in first place since May 29.

With a week to go in the regular season, the Pirates were on the verge of wrapping it up. A win by Pittsburgh or a loss by second-place St. Louis would assure the Pirates of the pennant. On Sunday, September 25, the Pirates were in Milwaukee, clinging to a 1–0 lead over the Braves. As the seventh inning was about to begin, they got word that the Cardinals had lost their game.

In their dugout, the Pirates shook hands with one another. Clemente wasn't able to join them, because he was just stepping in to hit. Clemente singled and, one out later, Hal Smith doubled. On Smith's hit, Clemente raced around the bases and scored, anxious to get back to the dugout so he could join his teammates in celebrating their pennant. The celebration continued in the locker room after the game, and it extended to Pittsburgh, where fans were ecstatic. In those days, baseball didn't have a multiple-round playoff system. The team with the best regular season record in each league went straight to the World Series. So, the World Series would take place in Pittsburgh for the first time since 1927.

When the Pirates got back to Pittsburgh after clinching the pennant in Milwaukee, they found themselves in a late-night victory parade. More than one hundred thousand fans had turned out to salute and cheer the Pirates. The players and coaches were driven through downtown Pittsburgh.

The Pirates still had a week left in the regular season, although the outcome of their final games didn't mean too much. The players focused on staying sharp for the upcoming championship series. Dick Groat, the team's star shortstop, had been out for several weeks after breaking his wrist when he was hit by a pitch. He came back in the final week, even though he risked lowering his batting average to the point that he might not lead the league. Groat was more interested in getting his batting eye back. On top of that, he had three hits in the final two games and still won the batting title.

Another player who finished strong was third baseman Don Hoak, who had hit .386 in the team's final 26 games. On the other hand, Clemente had cooled off near the end of the season. After being one of the challengers for the league batting-average title, he hit only .250 in his last 16 games.

The Pirates would need Clemente at his best in the World Series. Their opponents were the mighty New York Yankees, who had won their tenth American League pennant in the last twelve years. The Yankees were a slugging team, led by Mickey Mantle and Roger Maris. New York had some great pitchers too, including left-hander Whitey Ford.

The first two games of the best-of-seven series were at Forbes Field. In the opener, Pittsburgh had its ace, Vernon Law, on the mound, and he retired all three New York batters in the top of the first inning. The Pirates knocked in several runs in the bottom half. Two runs were already in when Clemente came to the plate and delivered a single that scored Bob Skinner. The

Yankees never caught up, and Pittsburgh won the game, 6–4.

The next two games were disasters for the Pirates. Mickey Mantle had two home runs and five RBIs to lead New York to a 16–3 win in game two. Clemente had two hits for the Pirates, but they didn't make much difference in a game like this one.

The series then shifted to Yankee Stadium in New York. Mantle had another big game, with four hits, one of which was a home run. But he wasn't the only Yankee playing well. Bobby Richardson hit a grand slam home run in the first inning. He later drove in two more runs, setting a World Series record with six RBIs in one game. On the mound, Whitey Ford held the Pirates to four hits (one by Clemente) and won, 10–0.

Blowouts like these two games could devastate a team. The Pirates, however, refused to give in. They won the fourth game of the series, 3–2, scoring all of their runs in the fifth inning. Clemente wasn't involved in the rally, but he did have a single in the next inning.

The last time the Pirates had been in the World Series, in 1927, their opponents were the New York Yankees. With its Murderer's Row team that included Babe Ruth and Lou Gehrig, the Yankees swept the Pirates, winning all four games.

The next day, Pittsburgh won again. Clemente had a run-scoring single in the third inning that gave the Pirates a 4–1 lead. They won the game, 5–2. The Pirates now had a lead of three games to two as the series shifted back to Pittsburgh. One more win would mean the championship for the Pirates.

But in the sixth game, they went up against Whitey Ford again. The Yankees' left-hander threw his second shutout of the series. Clemente had two hits, and the Pirates had a total of seven hits in the game, but they couldn't bunch the hits together enough to score even a single run. Meanwhile the Yankees hitters were busy, and New York won the game, 12–0.

In game seven, the entire championship was brought down to a single game. The pressure was on. The Pirates jumped out to a 4–0 lead, but the Yankees came back. Bill "Moose" Skowron got New York on the scoreboard with a home run in the fifth inning. In the sixth, the Yankees had another run in and two runners on base when Yogi Berra connected for a three-run home run. The Yankees now led, 5–4, and they increased the lead with two more runs in the eighth inning.

It was time for a Pirates comeback. Gino Cimoli led off with a single, and Bill Virdon hit a grounder toward Yankees shortstop Tony Kubek. The Forbes Field fans groaned. It looked like Kubek could field it and start a double play, snuffing out the rally. But the ball took a bad hop. Instead of bouncing up to where Kubek thought it would be, the ball came up higher and hit the shortstop in the throat. Kubek had to be removed from the game. The bad hop—which was a lucky break for the Pirates—meant that Pittsburgh had two runners on base with no outs. Dick Groat followed with a single that scored Cimoli to cut the Yankees' lead to 7–5. Bob Skinner put down a sacrifice bunt, putting runners at second and third. Rocky Nelson, who had earlier hit a two-run homer, flied to right. It wasn't deep enough to advance the runners, and the Pirates now had two out.

It was at this point that Clemente delivered his important infield single. Hal Smith followed with a three-run homer, and the Pirates took a 9–7 lead. Only three outs stood between the Pirates and the title. But this was no normal game—outs didn't come easily for either team. New York started the top of the ninth with two singles. Roger Maris popped out in foul territory, but Mantle singled to score Bobby Richardson and send Dale Long to third base.

The next batter was the dangerous Berra. He hit a sharp grounder down to Nelson at first base. Nelson fielded the ball and stepped on first for the second out of the inning. As this was happening, Long was running home from third. Nelson had no chance of throwing him out, but he did have a chance to tag Mantle. On Berra's grounder, Mantle had started toward second. After Nelson made the out, Mantle dashed back to first base. If Nelson could tag him for the third out before Long crossed the plate, the game would be over. But Nelson missed the tag. Mantle slid back into the base safely, and Long scored to tie the game, 9–9.

The Pirates finally got the last out of the inning, but the Pittsburgh fans were heartbroken. So were the players, including second baseman Bill Mazeroski, who would lead off the bottom of the ninth for the Pirates, although he wasn't even aware of it. "I was wondering how we'd get a run and didn't even know I was the next hitter," he recalled more than forty years later. "I was sitting on the bench when someone said, 'Maz, you're up.'"

The Pirates beat the Yankees in the 1960 World Series despite the Yankees scoring twice as many runs. New York scored 55 runs to Pittsburgh's 27. But the Pirates still won four games to the Yankees' three.

Mazeroski was known for his great fielding, not his hitting. But after what happened next, he will also be remembered for one swing of the bat. He looked at the first pitch in the bottom of the ninth, from New York's Bill Terry, for a ball. On the next one, he swung. The ball sailed high toward left field. Yankees

Yogi Berra (who switched between playing outfield and catcher) and Mickey Mantle ran toward it, but they looked up helplessly as the ball carried over the wall. The Pirates raced out of their dugout to greet Mazeroski as he completed his journey around the bases, giving Pittsburgh a world championship.

Clemente celebrated with his teammates in the locker room after the game. But he didn't join them when the party moved to a downtown hotel. Instead he went for a walk outside the stadium along with rejoicing fans, enjoying the victory in his own way.

# Chapter Six

# Battles On and Off the Diamond

Clemente was a big man in Pittsburgh after the Pirates won the World Series, but he was an even bigger man back in Puerto Rico. Returning to his homeland following the 1960 season, Clemente skipped the first half of the Puerto Rican League season but then joined the San Juan Senadores and helped them improve their record in the second half.

Even after he became a star in the major leagues, Clemente often played in the Puerto Rican League. He continued playing winter ball well past the time that he needed to keep his batting eye sharp because he felt an obligation to the people of his homeland, who otherwise wouldn't have a chance to see him play.

Clemente is perhaps the most inspirational figure the island has ever known, and he took that responsibility seriously. He frequently stood up for himself and his fellow Latino players, speaking out against injustices he thought occurred against them. He approached this in the same manner that he played— with a passion, sometimes an anger, that drove him on and off the field.

---

*66I didn't come into baseball originally to make money. I came into baseball to accomplish something and, in accomplishing something, I'm making money.*99
—ROBERTO CLEMENTE

---

Much of his anger was justified. Although the game became more open to Latinos after the breaking of the color barrier, certain attitudes and prejudices toward these players remained. Often, Latino players were accused of being lazy or faking an injury if they missed a game because they were hurt or ill. Clemente knew firsthand the feeling of being called a hypochondriac (someone who says he's ill or injured when he isn't). He suffered through many ailments in his career, and he burned when his manager or reporters didn't believe him when he said he was hurt.

A couple of medical practitioners have defended Clemente. One was Arturo García, a chiropractor in Puerto Rico who treated him. He said, "Roberto suffered plenty of pain during his career. He was born with a weak spine and had many ailments.

His pain didn't let him sleep. . . . But according to the American newspapers, he was just a hypochondriac."

Tony Bartirome played in the Pirates organization and later served as the team's trainer. "Every time [Clemente] was injured—*every time*—you would read this hypochondriac bit, about him always being injured, always being out of the lineup," said Bartirome. "Any person with lower back trouble will tell you what he went through. The muscles in his back used to get so rigid and tense that it took two and three days of constant moist heat, and rubbing, and adjusting, to loosen 'em. I've seen him go out on the field and play when he shouldn't have, when 99 percent of the players in both leagues wouldn't have gone *near* a ballpark."

Beyond the injuries and claims of hypochondria, Clemente maintained that Latino players often didn't receive the recognition they deserved. After helping the Pirates win the National League pennant and then the World Series championship, Clemente finished eighth in the voting for the league's MVP. Clemente thought he should have gotten more votes.

Two players who had finished ahead of Clemente for the 1960 MVP award were true stars of the game. Willie Mays and Chicago shortstop Ernie Banks had won the award the previous two years, respectively. Clemente's teammate, Dick Groat, won the award in 1960 after leading the league in batting average.

Roberto Clemente began playing for the Santurce Cangrejeros, or Crabbers, in Puerto Rico in 1952.

In 1960—Clemente's sixth year with Pittsburgh—the Pirates beat the New York Yankees to win the World Series. Clemente and his teammates rushed home plate when Bill Mazeroski hit the game-winning home run in game seven.

Teammate and fellow Pirates star Willie Stargell congratulates Clemente after a
home run.

Clemente was the leadoff batter for the National League in the 1964 All-Star Game, played at Shea Stadium, home of the New York Mets. It was his fifth appearance in the Midsummer Classic. He and the rest of the National League players celebrated the league's sixth win in seven All-Star Games.

Clemente was a standout player in the field as well as at the plate. He won the Gold Glove award twelve times in his career.

In 1970 the Pirates held a special Roberto Clemente night. Here, Roberto visits with his wife, Vera, and their sons, Enrique, Luis, and Roberto Jr.

Clemente smacked his 3,000th hit—a double—on September 30, 1972.

After the 3,000th hit, Clemente tipped his hat to acknowledge the cheering crowd as he stood on second base.

Clemente chose the number 21 because he had twenty-one letters in his full name: Roberto Clemente Walker.

THE GREAT ONE®

A larger-than-life statue of Clemente stands outside Pittsburgh's Three Rivers Stadium. The statue—and the team—moved to PNC Park in 2001.

Another Pittsburgh player, Don Hoak, finished second, and many people thought that Clemente was more deserving of the award than Hoak. Those voting for the MVP, however, often look at how a player did down the stretch. The fact that Hoak finished strong in 1960 while Clemente tailed off a bit may have had much to do with that.

Given the challenges Clemente faced, it's not surprising that he had a difficult relationship with the press. Phil Musick was a reporter who covered the Pittsburgh Pirates during the final years of Clemente's career. He said, "[Clemente] was anything but perfect. He was vain, occasionally arrogant. . . . Mostly, he acted as if the world had just declared all-out war on Roberto Clemente, when in fact it lavished him with an affection few men ever know."

Even so, Musick grew to admire the talented player. "Through all of his battles . . . there was about him an undeniable charisma," Musick added. "Perhaps that was his true essence—he won so much of your attention and affection that you demanded of him what no man can give, perfection."

Clemente's frustration about the MVP award after the 1960 season led him to work even harder the next year. "I made up my mind I'd win the batting title in 1961 for the first time," he said.

Clemente did exactly that, leading the National League with a .351 batting average. He also hit 23 home runs, scored

100 runs, and drove in 89 runs. On defense, he led National League outfielders with 27 assists. He won a Gold Glove for his fielding excellence for the first time. But despite the great season by Clemente, the Pirates fell in the standings, all the way to sixth place.

One of the highlights of the 1961 season came in July, when Clemente was the starting right fielder for the National League in both All-Star Games. The first All-Star Game took place in San Francisco. The game was scoreless in the second inning when Clemente hit a long fly to right. Roger Maris almost caught it, but the ball bounced off his glove and then off the fence. Clemente made it all the way to third with a triple and then scored the first run of the game on a sacrifice fly by Bill White.

In the fourth inning, Clemente hit a sacrifice fly to bring home Willie Mays and make the score 2–0 for the National League. The American League tied the score and then took the lead with a run in the top of the tenth inning. But the National League came back. Willie Mays drove home Hank Aaron with a double to tie the game. After Frank Robinson was hit by a pitch, Clemente came to the plate and singled to right-center field. The hit scored Mays and won the game for the National League.

The following year, Clemente continued to produce a batting average of more than .300 and emerged as the best player on the Pirates. Another great player, Willie Stargell, joined the team late in the 1962 season. An outfielder like Clemente, Stargell became a great home run hitter.

In Puerto Rico, Clemente played winter ball less often. He skipped the 1962–1963 season altogether. It was the first time he hadn't played in the Puerto Rican League other than the time he was in the Marine Reserves in 1958–1959.

In the National League in 1963, Clemente had another good year, producing a batting average of .320 and hitting 17 home runs. The Pirates had a big drop as a team, however, finishing in eighth place out of ten teams.

Clemente was back for a full season with San Juan in 1963–1964. He was in a battle to lead the league in batting average with Orlando Cepeda and Tony Oliva. Cepeda, a native of Puerto Rico, was already establishing himself as a star in the major leagues. Oliva, who was from Cuba, had played briefly for the Minnesota Twins at the end of the previous two seasons.

Clemente and Oliva played in separate leagues in the majors. Each player led his league in batting average in 1964 and 1965, Oliva for the Minnesota Twins in the American League and Clemente for the Pittsburgh Pirates in the National League.

Clemente's San Juan team finished third during the regular season, but the Senadores won the league playoffs. They represented Puerto Rico in the International Series, which was played in Managua, Nicaragua, where Clemente was popular with the fans.

The International Series in early 1964 gave Clemente a chance to visit Nicaragua for the first time. In the course of the series, he developed a fondness for the country and its people.

During the 1964 season, two stars of the previous winter led their leagues in batting average. Tony Oliva, playing his first full season in the majors, led the American League with a .323 average, and he credits his winter-league experience with helping his development as a hitter. Meanwhile Clemente's .339 average was good for his second National League batting title.

The winter of 1964–1965 was an eventful one for Clemente: He married Vera Cristina Zabala. Like Clemente, Vera was from Carolina, although the two didn't meet until a year before their marriage. She had attended the University of Puerto Rico and was a secretary at Puerto Rico's Government Development Bank. After their marriage, Roberto and Vera moved into a large home in Rio Piedras, just outside of San Juan.

*66 Roberto played just as hard in Puerto Rico as he did in the majors. He felt very strongly about pleasing the local fans and did not want to let them down. 99*

—VERA CLEMENTE,
ROBERTO CLEMENTE'S WIFE

Clemente also began managing in the Puerto Rican Leagues. In December 1964, Clemente took over as manager of the San Juan Senadores. He still played, although less often. In his first game as manager, Clemente had two doubles off Dennis McLain of Mayaguez. "He drove in two runs with his second double and raced home on a wild throw, but twisted his left ankle slightly and left the game," reported Miguel J. Frau in the *Sporting News.*

Clemente later suffered a more serious injury. He was mowing the lawn at his home when a rock flew out of the mower and hit his thigh. He missed several games as a player, but when the league's All-Star Game was played, Clemente felt obligated to make an appearance. He pinch-hit and singled, but as he ran to first, he aggravated the injury. "I felt my thigh ligament pop and something like water draining inside my leg," he said. Clemente had partially severed a ligament in his thigh, and he had to have it operated on.

The Pirates had a new manager, Harry Walker, in 1965. Clemente had often battled with his previous manager, Danny Murtaugh, who wasn't always supportive when Clemente claimed to be injured. (Murtaugh would manage the Pirates several more times, and eventually the two got along better.)

During the 1965 season, Clemente became a dad for the first time. In August Vera flew back to Puerto Rico to give birth to Roberto Jr. Ever proud of his heritage, Clemente thought it was important that his children were born in Puerto Rico.

Under Walker in 1965, the team began poorly, losing 24 of their first 33 games. The injury from the previous winter, along with a fever, left Clemente weak, and he also got off to a slow start. The Pirates went on a 12-game winning streak, however, lifting Pittsburgh in the standings. Clemente got hot over this stretch, hitting .458 during the team's winning streak.

Although the Pirates never overcame their slow start and weren't in the hunt for the pennant, they did finish third. Clemente led the league in batting average (.329) for the second year in a row and the third time in his career. He seemed to be at the peak of his abilities.

# Chapter Seven

# A Most Valuable Player

Clemente never stopped trying to improve. Little by little, he began to increase his walk total. As he got older, he got away from some of his bad ball hitting. He still wasn't walking as much as some of the real sluggers, but he knew that getting on base any way he could was important.

Early in the 1966 season, the Pirates were in Chicago, trailing the Cubs by a run. Clemente came to bat with two out and no one on base in the ninth inning. Cubs reliever Ted Abernathy got two strikes on Clemente. The Pirates were on the verge of losing.

But Clemente remained patient. Abernathy's next three pitches were outside the strike zone, and Clemente layed off them. The count was full. Clemente stayed alive by fouling off the next eight pitches. Finally Abernathy missed again and Clemente went to first base with a walk. Willie Stargell followed with a double, and Clemente came home with the tying run. Pittsburgh won the game in extra innings.

The win kept the Pirates in first place. Pittsburgh got off to a good start in 1966, and the Pirates stayed in the pennant race all season. Clemente was leading the way for the team. In addition to getting on base by a hit or a walk, he started hitting for more power. His home run total had dropped in recent years, but in 1966 that number started to rise.

### SOLID FOOTING

Clemente claimed that one of the reasons he hit so well at Forbes Field in 1966 was because the texture of the batter's box changed. "For years, I have been pleading with somebody in charge at Forbes Field to put clay instead of sand in the batter's box," he said. "Sand causes your feet to slip. Clay gives you a chance to keep your feet solid. So all I got for years was sand and more sand. Batters would dig holes. I come to bat and scrape dirt to cover up the holes. Suddenly, this year, they put clay in the batter's box. Now I have a firm footing. Now I can get a toehold."

During a road trip in May, the Pirates were struggling and Clemente was feeling tired. Manager Harry Walker gave him a few games off to rest. Clemente and the Pirates came back strong when the team got back to Forbes Field. In a Memorial Day doubleheader against the Cubs, Clemente had a home run in each game, lifting his season total to five. In the second game, he threw out George Altman at the plate. Altman was trying to score from first on a double, but Clemente fired a one-hop throw to home from deep right field to nail Altman. Chicago was already ahead, 3–0, and Clemente's great throw kept them from increasing their lead. The Pirates came back to win the game, giving them a sweep of the doubleheader.

With 28 hits, Clemente had a .444 batting average during Pittsburgh's 16-game home stand. He hit 6 home runs and drove in 19 runs during that stretch. Several of his home runs were memorable. Two cleared the wall in right center field between an on-field monument for former Pirates owner Barney Dreyfuss and a light tower, where the distance from home plate is listed as 436 feet. A few days later, Clemente hit a three-run homer to right field in the bottom of the eighth. Pittsburgh had been trailing in the game, 4–2, but Clemente's blast gave them a 5–4 win. Willie Stargell was also hot during this period, and the Pirates won 11 of 16 games.

Other good things were happening to Clemente at this time. For the second year in a row, he and Vera had a baby. Once again, Vera flew back to Puerto Rico and had a boy, named Luis Roberto, in June.

Manager Harry Walker rested Clemente several times during the 1966 season, giving him one or more games off. Clemente always did well following the rest. "A day off is like three days' rest in bed to me," said Clemente. "Two days off is like a week's vacation."

Pittsburgh faced tough competition for the top spot in the National League from the San Francisco Giants and Los Angeles Dodgers. (Like the Giants, the Dodgers had moved to the West Coast after the 1957 season.) At the end of August, the Pirates and Giants were tied for first. On September 2, Clemente had a big hit that helped Pittsburgh beat the Cubs and take over sole possession of first place. He hit a three-run homer off Chicago's Ferguson Jenkins to put the Pirates ahead, 4–0. It was the 2,000th hit of his career. It was also his 23rd homer of the year, which tied his previous career high. In addition, it gave him 101 runs batted in for the season. It was the first time he had ever reached 100 RBIs.

Clemente credited his teammates with their ability to get on base for having so many opportunities to drive in runs. "I finally have some players ahead of me who get on base," he said. "In other years, I would come to bat with a man on first or nobody on."

Clemente was a strong candidate for the National League MVP award. Sandy Koufax, the great left-handed pitcher for the Dodgers, was his main competition. The Pirates and Dodgers met for a big series in Los Angeles in mid-September. The Dodgers took two out of three games from the Pirates. In one of them, Koufax won his twenty-fourth game of the season.

Los Angeles went on to win the pennant, and the Pirates finished in third place, behind the Dodgers and Giants. It was a disappointing finish for Pittsburgh, since they had held first place during much of August and through the first third of September.

Reading was a way for Clemente to relax, with his favorites being history books and comic books. "The comics are for laughs, and the history for improvement of the mind," he said.

But after the season ended, Clemente found something to celebrate. In November the results of the MVP voting were announced. In another close race, Clemente edged out Sandy Koufax for the award.

Clemente had finished the season with a batting average of .317 and had 29 home runs and 119 runs batted in. He was second to Hank Aaron in RBIs. It was gratifying for Clemente to win the award. He still remembered how hurt he felt by finishing eighth in the MVP balloting in 1960. Capturing the award took away some of that sting.

In the off-season, Clemente stayed busy. In addition to playing and managing in the Puerto Rican League, he served as a scout for the Pirates, keeping an eye out for young Puerto Rican players. He also invested in real estate in the San Juan area and even opened a restaurant, El Carretero, which means "Man of the Road."

# Chapter Eight

# The Pride of Pittsburgh

Clemente didn't play winter baseball after the 1966 season. Luckily his fellow Puerto Ricans still had a chance to see him play when the Pirates held some of their final spring training games on the island just before the opening of the 1967 season.

Before the Pirates-Yankees exhibition game in San Juan, Clemente was honored and received a huge silver tray as a gift. He also got a kiss on the cheek from Maria Feliso Seda, who was Miss Puerto Rico and also the daughter of a Yankees scout in Puerto Rico, Jose Seda.

One of the games was against the New York Yankees. The Yankees were no longer a great team; they had finished in last place the previous season. But they still had some of their stars.

The Puerto Rican fans gave nice ovations to Whitey Ford, who pitched two innings, and Mickey Mantle, who hit a home run in the game. Their favorite star, though, was still Roberto Clemente. Clemente had two hits and scored two runs in the game as Pittsburgh beat the Yankees, 9–3.

Clemente was coming off a season that would be tough to top. But he did just that in 1967. He led the league with a .357 batting average. It was his third batting title in four years and his fourth overall. "Winning the batting title is something you do yourself," said Clemente. "You don't get any help."

In addition to his 209 hits, Clemente walked or was hit by a pitch more than 40 times, and his on-base percentage was .400. It was the first season in his career that he reached base 40 percent of the time. Despite another great season by Clemente, the Pirates finished in sixth place. Clemente played occasionally in the Puerto Rican League during the winter of 1967–1968 and had a batting average of .382.

Had the Pirates done better in 1967, Clemente likely would have received the MVP award again. Those who vote on the award often favor players on teams that finish first or at least are in contention for the pennant. Pittsburgh finished in sixth place, closer to last than first. In the end, Clemente finished third in the MVP balloting, behind Orlando Cepeda and Tim McCarver, who both played for the pennant-winning St. Louis Cardinals.

## BIGGEST BUT NOT BEST

Scoring runs wasn't a problem for the 1967 Pirates. Preventing runs was. A game in Cincinnati in mid-May was typical of the way the season went for the Pirates. Clemente had three home runs and a double, and he drove in all seven of Pittsburgh's runs. But the Reds still won the game, 8–7, in 10 innings. "It was my biggest game, but not my best game," said Clemente, indicating that he would have preferred a win. "My best game is when I drive in the winning run."

The start of the 1968 season was marred by tragedy. Shortly before the season opener, civil rights leader Martin Luther King Jr. was assassinated. The Pirates in particular felt the loss. The team had eleven players of color (either African Americans or black Latino players) out of the twenty-five players on its opening-day roster.

The players on the team didn't want to play until after King's funeral was held on Tuesday, April 9. Pittsburgh general manager Joe Brown agreed to cancel the Pirates' final spring-training game. The Pirates, however, were still scheduled to start the regular season in Houston on Monday, April 8. Brown said he would let the Houston Astros management decide whether or not to postpone the first two games of the series.

The Pittsburgh players were firm in their position. "We feel we cannot play these games out of respect to Dr. King, since we have the largest representation of Negroes in baseball on the Pirates," said Pittsburgh first baseman Donn Clendenon.

---

*I don't believe in color; I believe in people. I always respect everyone, and thanks to God my mother and my father taught me never to hate, never to dislike someone because of their color.*

—ROBERTO CLEMENTE

---

The players agreed unanimously that they would not play on Monday or Tuesday. Clemente and Pirates pitcher Dave Wickersham issued a joint statement. Wickersham is white, and his participation indicated that the issue went beyond skin color. The statement read, "We are doing this because we white and black players respect what Dr. King has done for mankind. Dr. King not only was concerned with Negros or whites but also with poor people. We owe this gesture to his memory and his ideals." Houston agreed to postpone the first two games until later in the season, and the Pirates and Astros played their first game on Wednesday, April 10.

Clemente hit a home run in the opener, but after that, he had problems hitting. His batting average at the end of May was only .222. He said he was having trouble swinging the bat because he had injured his right shoulder in a fall at his home in Puerto Rico in February 1968. He added that he might retire from baseball if the shoulder didn't improve.

For the third year in a row, the Pirates finished in sixth place even though Clemente improved over the last part of the season and finished with a batting average of .291. It was his lowest batting average since 1958, but he came back in 1969, determined to do better. He didn't play winter ball and rested his body. He felt good when spring training began in 1969, but then he hurt his left shoulder as he tried to make a diving catch. He went back to Puerto Rico so Arturo García could treat the injury.

Clemente was back in time for the beginning of the regular season, but for the second year in a row, he got off to a slow start. In the second half of May, after going hitless in the first game of a series in San Diego, his batting average had fallen to .225.

Clemente later said that a scary incident off the field had shaken his ability to focus on his game. A year after it happened, he told reporters that he had been kidnapped while in San Diego.

According to Clemente, he was walking back to the hotel where the Pirates were staying after picking up some dinner.

Four men forced him into a car at gunpoint. They took him to an isolated area and took his wallet and his All-Star Game ring. "This is where I figure they are going to shoot me and throw me in the woods," he told Pittsburgh writer Bill Christine more than a year after the incident. "They already had the pistol inside my mouth." Two of the men spoke Spanish, and Clemente talked to one of them in Spanish. After that, the men returned Clemente's money and ring and brought him back to his hotel. They even gave Clemente back the bag of chicken he had purchased. He said he didn't report the incident to the police.

Despite the harrowing event, Clemente finished the series in San Diego by getting three hits against the Padres. From then on, the hits came more often, and he raised his batting average. By mid-June his average was over .300, and it kept climbing. For a while, it looked like he might lead the league again. He didn't, but Clemente still finished the season with a batting average of .345. He was also able to celebrate the birth of another son, Enrique, in 1969.

Clemente was back to his old self, but his team was still falling short. Pittsburgh had thought its chances would be better in 1969. This was the year that the National and American leagues were split into two divisions each. Each league had two division champions, who played each other in a playoff series at the end of the season to determine who would go to the World

Series. But the Pirates managed only a third-place finish in 1969. After their championship in 1960, Pittsburgh had gone the rest of the 1960s without finishing first. Clemente and the Pirates hoped that the 1970s would be better.

# Chapter Nine

# Back to the Top

**D**anny Murtaugh was back for the third time as the Pirates manager in 1970. Another change in Pittsburgh in 1970 was where the games took place. A new stadium was being finished as the season opened, and the Pirates moved in a few months later. The new Three Rivers Stadium was near where the Allegheny and Monangahela rivers come together to form the Ohio River.

The Pirates got off to a poor start. By the end of May, they had lost more games than they had won. But then the team got hot in June.

The Pirates won the final seven games played at Forbes Field. The end of the historic stadium came with a Sunday doubleheader against the Cubs on June 28. The Pirates won both games, which put them within a few percentage points of the New York Mets for first place in the National League East Division. They went on the road, and by the time they returned home to their new stadium, the Pirates had first place to themselves.

Forbes Field had been the home of the Pirates since 1909. It was a historic stadium that was the site of several World Series. Many greats played for the Pirates at Forbes Field, including Honus Wagner, who is considered by some experts to be the best shortstop ever.

New York and Pittsburgh continued to fight for first through July, with the Chicago Cubs staying close. The Pirates were hanging in without Clemente. He was hit in the wrist with a pitch and, except for one pinch-running appearance, was out of the lineup for more than a week. He returned on August 8 and had a double and a home run against the Mets.

Later in August, Clemente had five hits in each of two straight games. The first one came on a Saturday in Los Angeles. Clemente already had four hits as he came to the plate in the top of the sixteenth inning. He singled, stole second, and later scored the go-ahead run as the Pirates beat the Dodgers, 2–1. The next day, the Pirates won again, 11–0. Clemente had five of Pittsburgh's 23 hits in the game.

Clemente had raised his average to .363, tops in the National League. But he played little in September because of a bad back, and he failed to win the batting title. Even without Clemente, the Pirates still won the National League East Division and advanced to the playoffs.

Their opponents were the Cincinnati Reds, champions of the West Division. The first team to win three games in this best-of-five-game series would win the National League pennant and go to the World Series. Unfortunately Pittsburgh had trouble hitting, scoring only three runs as they were swept in three games by the Reds.

## TWO LOVES

Soon after Three Rivers Stadium opened, the Pirates hosted Roberto Clemente Night before a crowd of more than 43,000 fans. "I began one life in 1934 when I was born in Puerto Rico and I began another life in 1955 when I began playing baseball in Pittsburgh," Clemente told the fans before the game. "I have had two loves. My family—my father and mother, my wife and my children—and my fans in Pittsburgh and Puerto Rico." In the game, Clemente had two singles and a walk. He also made two nice catches as Pittsburgh beat Houston, 11–0.

That winter Clemente played for the last time in the Puerto Rican League. Although he appeared in only three games during the regular season, he took part in the playoff series. In addition, Clemente managed the San Juan Senadores in 1970–1971. The Senadores' opening game that season was against Santurce, which was managed by two-time MVP Frank Robinson. Both Robinson and Clemente had been mentioned as possibilities to be the first black manager in the major leagues.

Frank Robinson later became the first black man to manage in the major leagues when he became a player-manager for the Cleveland Indians in 1975. Robinson was still managing in the majors thirty years later.

Clemente wasn't entirely sure that managing was right for him, however. He said he regretted having managed over the winter when he got off to a slow start with the Pirates in 1971. "My biggest mistake was managing in Puerto Rico that past winter," he said. "I had more responsibilities and did not get my rest. The long bus trips out of town, I have to make them because I am the manager. They take something out of me."

It was outfielder Willie Stargell who took the lead with Pittsburgh in 1971. He set a major league record by hitting 11 home runs in April, and he continued his great hitting through-out the year. Stargell finished the season with 48 home runs and 125 runs batted in.

Although Stargell had emerged as the team's star player, Clemente remained the team leader. He was receiving the recognition he had sought, and he was also showing he could continue playing with the same flair and hustle even as he approached his thirty-seventh birthday. Clemente got off to a bad start with his hitting during the first month, but he got hot in May and went on to finish the season with a .341 batting average.

He was still awesome in the field too. In mid-June, Clemente preserved a shutout for Steve Blass, and a victory for the Pirates, on back-to-back plays. Pittsburgh held a 1–0 lead over Houston in the bottom of the eighth inning. The Astros had a runner on first with one out when Cesar Cedeno hit a soft liner to right field. Clemente hustled in and made a sliding catch of the ball before it could hit the turf. The next batter, Bob Watson, hit a much harder drive toward the corner in right. Clemente raced toward the ball and made a twisting leap, grabbing the ball and robbing Watson of a two-run homer. Clemente crashed into the wall, bruising his ankle and elbow and cutting his knee. Astros manager Harry Walker, who had managed Clemente in Pittsburgh, said it was the greatest catch Clemente ever made.

Because of Clemente's amazing catch, the Pirates maintained their lead and then padded it with two more runs in the ninth. Blass finished with a 3–0 win but said, "That shutout belongs to Clemente."

The win gave the Pirates a 3½-game lead over the New York Mets and St. Louis Cardinals. Pittsburgh increased its first-place lead to 9½ games at the All-Star break in July.

The Pirates had several players in the All-Star Game, including two starters—Willie Stargell in left field and Dock Ellis, who pitched. Clemente didn't start, but he entered the game as a replacement for Willie Mays in the fourth inning. Later in the game, Clemente homered. It was his first home run in an All-Star Game. Unfortunately the American League still pulled off a win.

Clemente's home run in the 1971 All-Star Game in Detroit was one of six hits in the game by a future member of the National Baseball Hall of Fame. The others were hit by Johnny Bench, Hank Aaron, Reggie Jackson, Frank Robinson, and Harmon Killebrew.

Clemente and the Pirates had another chance for national attention that fall. After winning the East Division, the Pirates faced San Francisco in the league playoffs, which were a three-out-of-five series. The Giants won the first game, but Pittsburgh came back to win the second game, 9–4. Bob Robertson was the star, hitting three homers for the Pirates in the game. But Clemente contributed too. He had a single to drive in a run and later scored as Pittsburgh broke the game open with four runs in the seventh.

In the third game of the series, Clemente had a two-run single in the bottom of the first to put Pittsburgh ahead, 2–1. The Pirates went on to win the game and were only a win away from the World Series.

The next game was tied in the sixth inning when Clemente singled in a run to put Pittsburgh ahead. He scored later in the inning when Al Oliver hit a three-run homer. The Pirates won the game, 9–5, and the playoff series.

In the World Series, the Pirates' opponents were the Baltimore Orioles, a team that had a pitching staff with four twenty-game winners. The Pirates jumped on one of those pitchers, Dave McNally, for three runs early in the first game of the series. Pittsburgh's starter, Dock Ellis, couldn't hold the lead, however, and the Orioles won, 5–3.

Baltimore won again in the next game, 11–3. Clemente had a double and a single for the second game in a row, but his team was still behind in the series.

The World Series shifted to Pittsburgh for game three, and the Pirates desperately needed a win. They sent Steve Blass to the mound to face Baltimore's Mike Cuellar. Pittsburgh put runners at first and third with no out in the bottom of the first. Clemente then grounded into a fielder's choice, but a run scored on the play. Pittsburgh had a 1–0 lead. The Pirates got another run in the sixth, but Frank Robinson homered for the Orioles to cut the lead to 2–1.

Mike Cuellar, who started two games against the Pirates in the 1971 World Series, had briefly pitched for Clemente's San Juan team in the Puerto Rican League the previous winter.

Clemente led off the bottom of the seventh by grounding back to Cuellar. Clemente hustled down to first so hard that Cuellar hurried his throw and threw wildly. Clemente reached base on the error, and, after Stargell walked, Bob Robertson hit a three-run homer. Blass was outstanding for the Pirates, allowing only three hits as Pittsburgh won the game, 5–1.

The next game was the first night game in the history of the World Series. Traditionally, World Series games had been afternoon contests. The Orioles got off to an early lead with three runs in the top of the first. Pittsburgh came back with two in the bottom of the inning, and the Pirates rallied again in the third. With one out, Richie Hebner singled. Clemente then hit a long drive to right. It cleared the fence and looked like a home run to put the Pirates ahead again. But one of the umpires ruled that the ball was foul. The other umpires then got together and had a long discussion, trying to decide if that had been the correct call. Eventually they ruled that it was. The ball was foul, and Clemente had to resume his at bat.

Clemente couldn't come up with another long ball, but he did single, sending Hebner to second. One out later, Al Oliver singled, scoring Hebner and tying the game. The score stayed at 3–3 until the Pirates pushed another run across in the seventh inning. Pittsburgh won the game, 4–3, and tied the World Series, 2–2.

The Pirates won again the next day as Nelson Briles held the Orioles to two hits. Clemente had a run-scoring single in the fifth inning to cap Pittsburgh's scoring as the Pirates won, 4–0.

The World Series shifted back to Baltimore, but Pittsburgh had the lead in the series. One more win would give the Pirates the championship.

Just as he had done in the 1960 World Series, Clemente had at least one hit in each of the games. In the sixth game, he continued his hot hitting. With two outs in the top of the first, he tripled off the fence in left-center field. Unfortunately outfielder

Willie Stargell struck out and stranded Clemente at third base.

By the time Clemente came up again, in the third inning, the Pirates had a 1–0 lead. Clemente made the score 2–0 by hitting a home run to right field. Pittsburgh carried the lead into the late innings and was on the verge of winning the World Series. But the Orioles didn't quit. They tied the game in the seventh. In the bottom of the tenth inning, Brooks Robinson hit a sacrifice fly that scored Frank Robinson, giving Baltimore the win and extending the series to a seventh game.

Blass and Cuellar matched up again in the final game, and both pitchers were sharp. Cuellar retired the first eleven Pittsburgh batters. Then Clemente stepped into the batter's box with two out in the fourth. Cuellar threw him a high curveball, and Clemente drove it to left-center field. The ball carried over the fence. Clemente's second home run of the series gave Pittsburgh a 1–0 lead.

The Pirates got another run in the eighth inning, which they needed. In the bottom of the eighth, Baltimore got the first two runners on base. Blass was able to work out of the jam with only one run scoring, leaving Pittsburgh in the lead. Blass retired the Orioles in order in the last of the ninth. Clemente's homer had given the Pirates a lead they never gave up. Pittsburgh won the game, 2–1, and the Pirates were again champions of the world.

The Pirates had a number of pitchers who stood out in the series, but when the voting was complete for the outstanding player of the World Series, the award went to Clemente. He had 12 hits, including two home runs, for a .414 batting average in the seven games. Clemente was finally getting the respect he'd longed for as a youngster.

# Chapter Ten

# A Final Milestone

Clemente had played in the All-Star Game and the World Series, had won the MVP award, and had led the National League in batting average four times. But he still had another milestone in his sights. "I would like to get 3,000 hits," he said in 1971.

To this point, only ten players had reached that level. Hank Aaron and Willie Mays had both done it in 1970. Clemente wanted to join this prestigious group. He had 2,882 hits at the end of 1971, and another full season would probably be enough for him to reach that magic number.

Bill Virdon, who had played on the 1960 Pirates championship team, was now managing the Pirates. Danny Murtaugh, who had heart problems, retired after the 1971 season. Virdon had also taken over as manager of the San Juan Senadores from Clemente in the winter of 1971–1972. Clemente attended some games during the winter, but he didn't play. His career in the Puerto Rican League was over.

Clemente was saving his strength for Pittsburgh. The Pirates had a rough start and were in last place in May. They climbed in the standings, however, and by the last half of June had taken over first place for good.

---

### HORSING AROUND

Late in Clemente's career, Pirates owner John Galbreath named a racehorse in his honor. The equine Roberto ended up winning the 1972 Epsom Derby.

---

Clemente was also doing well even though he had an intestinal virus in June that caused him to miss a few games. By the end of June, his batting average was .315, and he was making good progress toward the mark of 3,000 hits. On July 9, he got his 78th hit of the season, leaving him only 40 short.

Then the virus returned, and Clemente left the Pirates to go back to Pittsburgh for treatment. He was out of the lineup for two weeks, then came back and got a big hit in a Pirates win on July 23. Clemente was also dealing with strained tendons in both heels, and he missed another four weeks. Over a forty-game span between July 9 and August 22, he started only one game.

Fortunately, the Pirates were still playing well and opened up a big lead in the National League East Division. But the illness and injuries had slowed Clemente in his drive toward 3,000 hits.

Clemente was voted by fans to start in the All-Star Game in 1972. Because of his ailments, however, he didn't play.

He was planning on playing again in 1973, so it didn't seem necessary for him to reach the milestone before the end of the season. The fans, on the other hand, wanted to see him do it in 1972, to make sure that he got it done. After all, no one ever knew what would happen in the off-season.

At the end of August, Clemente had thirty hits to go. He hit well in September and was within striking distance by the final week of the season. On Thursday night, September 28, he got his 2,999th hit off Steve Carlton of the Phillies. Because the game was in Philadelphia, Clemente was taken out before he batted again. That way he could get his 3,000th hit before the home fans.

The Pirates opened a series against the New York Mets in Pittsburgh on Friday night. Clemente was hitless in the first game. The next afternoon, he struck out in the first inning. The game was scoreless when Clemente came up again, leading off the fourth.

---

### A PREMATURE SIGNAL

Clemente thought he had his 3,000th hit off Tom Seaver of the Mets on September 29. In the first inning, he hit a chopper up the middle. Second baseman Ken Boswell bobbled the ball, and Clemente reached first. An *H* to signify a hit—rather than an error—flashed on the scoreboard. But it was a mistake. The official scorer ruled an error on the play, and Clemente had to wait until the next day to get his 3,000th hit.

---

Clemente hit a long fly toward left-center field. The ball hit the fence on one bounce, and Clemente cruised into second with a double, the 3,000th hit of his career. The Pittsburgh fans stood and applauded Clemente, who raised his cap to show his appreciation. Clemente's hit started a three-run rally, and the Pirates won the game, 5–0. Bill Mazeroski pinch-hit for Clemente in the fifth inning.

Clemente played in only one of Pittsburgh's final three games as he rested for the playoffs. The Pirates played Cincinnati and looked like they were on their way back to the World Series. Pittsburgh carried a 3–2 lead into the last of the ninth inning of the decisive fifth game. But Johnny Bench tied the game with a home run, and the Reds later scored the winning run on a wild pitch. The Pirates lost, and their season was over.

As usual, Clemente went back to Puerto Rico. Although he didn't play baseball, Clemente became manager of a Puerto Rican team that went to the Amateur Baseball World Series in Nicaragua. The Puerto Rican team finished third in the tournament. Clemente was back home again when a massive earthquake struck Managua, the capital of Nicaragua, on December 23. Clemente had made friends during his visits to Nicaragua. He was concerned about the people there and wanted to help.

Clemente returned from the Amateur Baseball World Series in Nicaragua in early December. It was only a few weeks later that the earthquake struck Nicaragua.

Clemente got busy organizing a committee to raise money and get other items, such as medicine and food, that could be sent to Nicaragua. Through Christmas, Clemente worked on the relief efforts. Concerned that the supplies weren't reaching the people who needed them, he decided he would go on one of the cargo planes that were flying the supplies to the stricken area.

He planned to leave on Sunday, December 31, the final day of 1972. The flight was delayed. A little after 9 P.M., as others in Puerto Rico were celebrating New Year's Eve, the plane took off. Besides Clemente, four other people were on board.

---

*If you have an opportunity to make things better and you don't do that, you are wasting your time on this earth.*

—ROBERTO CLEMENTE

---

Almost immediately, the plane had problems, and the pilot tried to return to the San Juan airport. Before the plane could make it back, however, it crashed into the Atlantic Ocean about a mile from the coast.

The fate of the people on board was not immediately known. But quickly it became clear. The five men on the plane, including Roberto Clemente, were dead. Puerto Rico had lost its greatest baseball hero.

# The Legend Lives On

**D**ivers searched the plane wreckage for Clemente's body, but it was never found. Memorial services were held in Pittsburgh and Puerto Rico. People everywhere—not just baseball fans—mourned the loss of a great humanitarian.

Clemente had played eighteen seasons in the major leagues and had a career batting average of .317. He led the league in batting average four times. In addition to the MVP award he received in 1966, he finished in the top ten of the MVP voting five other times. He was recognized for his defensive brilliance with twelve Gold Gloves.

All three of Clemente's sons played baseball professionally in the minor leagues. Roberto Jr., Luis, and Enrique never reached the major leagues, but one of Clemente's nephews, Edgard Clemente, did make it, playing briefly for the Colorado Rockies and Anaheim Angels.

Normally a player can't be inducted into the National Baseball Hall of Fame until at least five years have passed since he stopped playing. However, because of the circumstances, an exception was made for Clemente. A special election was held, and he received enough votes to be elected. In the summer of 1973, Clemente became the first Latin American player to be inducted into the Hall of Fame. One of the other players inducted that year was Monte Irvin, whom Clemente had watched and admired as a young boy in Puerto Rico.

There were other honors. The Pirates displayed number 21, Clemente's number, on the left sleeve of their uniforms during the 1973 season in memory of him. An award, established in 1971 to honor a player for his accomplishments on and off the field, was renamed the Roberto Clemente Award. Willie Stargell, Clemente's former teammate, received the award in 1974. Other recipients include Rod Carew, Pete Rose, Cal Ripken Jr., and Sammy Sosa.

A dream Clemente had was to establish Sports City for young people in Puerto Rico. He had a vision of a place where young people could come and play as well as read and learn other skills they would need in life. Vera Clemente continued her husband's work, and the large sports complex was built. Over the next thirty years, hundreds of thousands of kids took part in its programs. Some of them became stars in the major leagues, including Juan Gonzalez, Bernie Williams, and Ivan Rodriguez. Clemente's son Luis serves as president and chief executive officer of Sports City.

Although he's gone, all sorts of reminders of Clemente still exist, like statues of him in Puerto Rico and Pittsburgh. More than anything, Roberto Clemente left behind memories of how he played the game on the field and how he lived his life off it.

# PERSONAL STATISTICS

**Name:**

Roberto Clemente Walker

**Nicknames:**

Momen

**Born:**

August 18, 1934

**Died:**

December 31, 1972

**Height:**

5' 11"

**Weight:**

175 lbs.

**Batted:**

Right

**Threw:**

Right

# BATTING STATISTICS

| Year | Team | Avg | G | AB | Runs | Hits | 2B | 3B | HR | RBI | SB |
|------|------|-----|---|----|----|----|----|----|----|-----|----|
| 1955 | PIT | .255 | 124 | 474 | 48 | 121 | 23 | 11 | 5 | 47 | 2 |
| 1956 | PIT | .311 | 147 | 543 | 66 | 169 | 30 | 7 | 7 | 60 | 6 |
| 1957 | PIT | .253 | 111 | 451 | 42 | 114 | 17 | 7 | 4 | 30 | 0 |
| 1958 | PIT | .289 | 140 | 519 | 69 | 150 | 24 | 10 | 6 | 50 | 8 |
| 1959 | PIT | .296 | 105 | 432 | 60 | 128 | 17 | 7 | 4 | 50 | 2 |
| 1960 | PIT | .314 | 144 | 570 | 89 | 179 | 22 | 6 | 16 | 94 | 4 |
| 1961 | PIT | .351 | 146 | 572 | 100 | 201 | 30 | 10 | 23 | 89 | 4 |
| 1962 | PIT | .312 | 144 | 538 | 95 | 168 | 28 | 9 | 10 | 74 | 6 |
| 1963 | PIT | .320 | 152 | 600 | 77 | 192 | 23 | 8 | 17 | 76 | 12 |
| 1964 | PIT | .339 | 155 | 622 | 95 | 211 | 40 | 7 | 12 | 87 | 5 |
| 1965 | PIT | .329 | 152 | 589 | 91 | 194 | 21 | 14 | 10 | 65 | 8 |
| 1966 | PIT | .317 | 154 | 638 | 105 | 202 | 31 | 11 | 29 | 119 | 7 |
| 1967 | PIT | .357 | 147 | 585 | 103 | 209 | 26 | 10 | 23 | 110 | 9 |
| 1968 | PIT | .291 | 132 | 502 | 74 | 146 | 18 | 12 | 18 | 57 | 2 |
| 1969 | PIT | .345 | 138 | 507 | 87 | 175 | 20 | 12 | 19 | 91 | 4 |
| 1970 | PIT | .352 | 108 | 412 | 65 | 145 | 22 | 10 | 14 | 60 | 3 |
| 1971 | PIT | .341 | 132 | 522 | 82 | 178 | 29 | 8 | 13 | 86 | 1 |
| 1972 | PIT | .312 | 102 | 378 | 68 | 118 | 19 | 7 | 10 | 60 | 0 |
| | Totals | .317 | 2,433 | 9,454 | 1,416 | 3,000 | 440 | 166 | 240 | 1,305 | 83 |

Key: Avg: batting average; G: games; AB: at bats; 2B: doubles; 3B: triples; HR: home runs; RBI: runs batted in; SB: stolen bases

# FIELDING STATISTICS

| Year | Team | Pos | G | C | PO | A | E | DP | FLD% |
|------|------|-----|-----|-----|-----|-----|-----|-----|-------|
| 1955 | PIT | OF | 118 | 271 | 253 | 18 | 6 | 5 | .978 |
| 1956 | PIT | OF | 139 | 291 | 274 | 17 | 13 | 2 | .957 |
| | | 2B | 2 | 2 | 1 | 1 | 1 | 0 | .667 |
| | | 3B | 1 | 2 | 0 | 2 | 1 | 0 | .667 |
| 1957 | PIT | OF | 109 | 281 | 272 | 9 | 6 | 1 | .979 |
| 1958 | PIT | OF | 135 | 334 | 312 | 22 | 6 | 3 | .982 |
| 1959 | PIT | OF | 104 | 239 | 229 | 10 | 13 | 1 | .948 |
| 1960 | PIT | OF | 142 | 265 | 246 | 19 | 8 | 2 | .971 |
| 1961 | PIT | OF | 144 | 283 | 256 | 27 | 9 | 5 | .969 |
| 1962 | PIT | OF | 142 | 288 | 269 | 19 | 8 | 1 | .973 |
| 1963 | PIT | OF | 151 | 250 | 239 | 11 | 11 | 2 | .958 |
| 1964 | PIT | OF | 154 | 302 | 289 | 13 | 10 | 2 | .968 |
| 1965 | PIT | OF | 145 | 304 | 288 | 16 | 10 | 1 | .968 |
| 1966 | PIT | OF | 154 | 335 | 318 | 17 | 12 | 3 | .965 |
| 1967 | PIT | OF | 145 | 290 | 273 | 17 | 9 | 4 | .970 |
| 1968 | PIT | OF | 131 | 306 | 297 | 9 | 5 | 1 | .984 |
| 1969 | PIT | OF | 135 | 240 | 226 | 14 | 5 | 1 | .980 |
| 1970 | PIT | OF | 104 | 201 | 189 | 12 | 7 | 2 | .966 |
| 1971 | PIT | OF | 124 | 278 | 267 | 11 | 2 | 4 | .993 |
| 1972 | PIT | OF | 94 | 204 | 199 | 5 | 0 | 2 | 1.000 |
| | Total | | 2,373 | 4,966 | 4,697 | 269 | 142 | 42 | .972 |

Key: Pos: position; G: games; C: chances (balls hit to a position); PO: putouts; A: assists; E: errors; DP: double plays; FLD%: fielding percentage

# SOURCES

5  Jack Cassini, telephone interview with author, June 20, 2005.

6  Thomas E. Van Hyning, *Puerto Rico's Winter League: A History of Major League Baseball's Launching Pad* (Jefferson, NC: McFarland, 1995).

8  Monte Irvin, telephone interview with author, June 30, 2005.

8  Ibid.

8  "Roberto Hit Ten HRs in 'Day-Long' Slugfest," *The Sporting News*, July 6, 1960, 6.

9  Kal Wagenheim, *Clemente!* (New York: Praeger Publishers, 1973), 24.

9–10  Les Biederman, "Pride Pushes Clemente: 'I Can Hit With Best,'" *The Sporting News*, March 28, 1964, 11.

12  Les Biederman, "Clemente  The Player Who Can Do It All," The Sporting News, April 20, 1968, 11.

15  Jack Hernon, "Another Record for Rickey—14 Flyhawks on Bucs' List," *The Sporting News*, December 8, 1954, 20.

16  Buzzie Bavasi, e-mail message to author, June 3, 2005.

16–17  Ibid.

17  Phil Musick, *Who Was Roberto? A Biography of Roberto Clemente* (Garden City, NY: Doubleday, 1974), 81.

18  Musick, 89.

19  Ibid.

22  Cassini, telephone interview.

23  Musick, 97.

23  Bavasi, e-mail message.

24  Ibid.

25  Jack Hernon, "Backward Buccos Refuse to Go Overboard on Rookie," *The Sporting News*, January 12, 1955, 18.

28  Don Zimmer, interview with author, July 2, 2005.

28  Ibid.

29  Jack Hernon, "Clemente a Gem—in Need of Polish—B. R. Sizeup," *The Sporting News*, February 9, 1955, 4.

29  Jack Hernon, "Backward Buccos Refuse to Go Overboard on Rookie," *The Sporting News*, January 12, 1955, 18.

29–30  Jack Hernon, "Haney's Sizeup on Bob Clemente—'Much to Learn,'" *The Sporting News*, March 16, 1955, 30.

31–32  Jack Hernon, "Haney's Young Bucs Shaking off Buck Fever," *The Sporting News*, May 11, 1955, 11.

32  Les Biederman, "Clemente, Early Buc Ace, Says He's Better in Summer," *The Sporting News*, June 29, 1955, 26.

33  Cassini, telephone interview.

38  Oscar Ruhl, "Rickey Rates Clemente as Top Draft Dandy," *The Sporting News*, March 20, 1957, 15.

40  "Roberto Clemente Quotes by Baseball Almanac," *baseball-almanac.com*, n.d., http://www.baseball-almanac.com/quotes/roberto_clemente quotes.shtml (January 18, 2006).

40  "Clemente, Best When Ailing, Reports Late with Backache," *The Sporting News*, March 13, 1957, 10.

41  Robert Dvorchak, "One more push to realize Clemente's dream of Sports City," *Pittsburgh Post-Gazette*, Monday, August 16, 2004, http://post-gazette.com/pg/04229/362393.stm (January 18, 2006).

45  Les Biederman, "Roberto Clemente," *The Sporting News*, May 25, 1960, 21.

46  Harry Keck, "Clemente 'Cool' Corsair with Keen Cutlass," *The Sporting News*, July 6, 1960, 5.

54  Bill Mazeroski, interview with author, July 9, 2002.

57  Les Biederman, "Clemente—The Player Who Can Do It All," *The Sporting News*, April 20, 1968, 11.

57–58  Wagenheim, 113–114.

58  Wagenheim, 143.

59  Musick, 14–15.

59  Les Biederman, "Clemente—The
    Player Who Can Do It All," *The
    Sporting News,* April 20, 1968, 11.

63  Thomas E. Van Hyning, "Hall of
    Famers Shine in Puerto Rico," *The
    National Pastime,* Society for American
    Baseball Research, 1992, 15.

63  Miguel J. Frau, "Puerto Rico: Senators
    Dip as Clemente Grabs Reins," *The
    Sporting News,* January 9, 1965, 27.

63  "Clemente May Have Trouble As
    Result of Thigh Injury," *The Sporting
    News,* February 13, 1965, 25.

66  Les Biederman, "Clemente Sinks Feet
    in Clay to Mold Stout Swat Figures,"
    *The Sporting News,* July 2, 1966, 8.

68  "When Roberto Rests, Rivals Better
    Beware," *The Sporting News,*
    September 10, 1966, 5.

68  Les Biederman, "Roberto's Bat Softens
    Rivals for Buc Raids," *The Sporting
    News,* September 17, 1966, 6.

69  "Reads Comics for Guffaws—History
    to Improve Mind," *The Sporting News,*
    July 6, 1960, 6.

72  Les Biederman, "Clemente—The
    Player Who Can Do It All," *The
    Sporting News,* April 20, 1968, 11.

73  "N. L. Player of the Week: Roberto
    Clemente," *The Sporting News,* June 3,
    1967, 23.

74  "Pirates Vote Delay in Memory of
    King," *The Sporting News,* April 20,
    1968, 11.

74  Musick, 111.

74  "Pirates Vote Delay in Memory of
    King," *The Sporting News,* April 20,
    1968, 11.

76  "Clemente Reveals Close Call with
    Kidnapers," *The Sporting News,*
    August 22, 1970, 24.

80  "Two Lives and Two Loves, Clemente
    Tells Buc Fans," *The Sporting News,*
    August 8, 1970, 13.

81  "Clemente Laments Managing," *The
    Sporting News,* May 15, 1971, 14.

83  Charley Feeney, "Greatest Catch? This
    One by Roberto Will Do," *The Sporting
    News,* July 3, 1971, 7.

89  Charley Feeney, "Clemente Sets 3,000
    Hits as Wish on 37th Birthday," *The
    Sporting News,* August 28, 1971, 9.

94  "Arriba Roberto!" *Sports Illustrated,*
    December 28, 1992, 114.

# BIBLIOGRAPHY

Bjarkman, Peter C. *Baseball with a Latin Beat: A History of the Latin American Game.* Jefferson, NC: McFarland, 1994.

Markusen, Bruce. *Roberto Clemente: The Great One.* Champaign, IL: Sports Pub., 1998.

Musick, Phil. *Who Was Roberto? A Biography of Roberto Clemente.* Garden City, NY: Doubleday, 1974.

Van Hyning, Thomas E. *Puerto Rico's Winter League: A History of Major League Baseball's Launching Pad.* Jefferson, NC: McFarland, 1995.

———. *The Santurce Crabbers: Sixty Seasons of Puerto Rican Winter League Baseball.* Jefferson, NC: McFarland, 1999.

Wagenheim, Cal. *Clemente!* New York: Praeger Publishers, 1973.

# WEBSITES

The Official Roberto Clemente Website

www.robertoclemente21.com

*This website includes a biography, career highlights, photos, memorabilia, personal/family information, and a newsletter.*

Pittsburgh Pirates: The Official Site

www.pirateball.com

*The official Pirates site has a ton of information, including a history section that tells about Clemente's years with the team.*

Retrosheet

www.retrosheet.org

*Retrosheet has play-by-play accounts of many major league baseball games that took place before 1984.*

# INDEX

## A

Aaron, Henry "Hank," 9, 12, 46–47, 60, 70, 83, 89
Abernathy, Ted, 65
All-Star Game, 38, 47
Almendares of Cuba, 27
Alston, Walter, 47
Altman, George, 67
Amateur Baseball World Series, 93
Amoros, Sandy, 18
Anaheim Angels, 95
Arecibo, 6
Arroyo, Luis "Tite," 39

## B

Baltimore Orioles, 84–87
Banks, Ernie, 58
Bartirome, Tony, 58
Bavasi, Emil "Buzzie," 12, 16, 22–24
Bell, Cool Papa, 11
Bench, Johnny, 83, 93
Berra, Yogi, 52–53, 55
Biederman, Les, 32
Blass, Steve, 41, 82, 85, 87
Boston Braves, 44
Boswell, Ken, 92
Bragan, Bobby, 35–37, 40
Briles, Nelson, 86
Brooklyn Dodgers, 10, 12–18, 22–24, 30–31. See also Los Angeles Dodgers
Brosnan, Jim, 37
Brown, Joe L., 40, 73
Brown, Willard "Ese Hombre," 11

## C

Caguas-Guayama Criollos, 12, 26–27, 35
Caguas-Rio Piedras, 38
Campanella, Roy, 9
Campanis, Al, 10, 12
Capeda, Orlando, 6
Capeda, Pedro "Perucho," 6
Carew, Rod, 96
Caribbean leagues, 5–6, 11

Caribbean Series, 4, 27–28
Carleton, Steve, 91
Carta Vieja, 28
Cassini, Jack, 5, 18–19, 22, 33
Castro, Fidel, 5
Cedeno, Cesar, 82
Cepeda, Orlando, 61, 72
Chicago Cubs, 37, 41, 44, 65, 67–68, 78–79
Christine, Bill, 76
Cimoli, Gino, 18, 47, 52–53
Cincinnati Reds, 36–37, 41–42, 45–46, 73, 80, 92
Clarkson, James "Buster," 11–12
Clemente, Edgard, 95
Clemente, Enrique, 76, 95
Clemente, Luis Roberto, 67, 95, 97
Clemente, Luisa Walker, 6–7
Clemente, Melchor, 6–7
Clemente, Roberto
  athletics, 7–8
  batting statistics, 99
  childhood, 6
  death, 94
  early baseball, 8–10
  fielding statistics, 100
  major league career, 29–97
  minor league career, 14–24
  personal statistics, 98
  Puerto Rican League baseball, 10–12, 25–28, 35, 38–40, 45, 56, 61–62, 63, 70, 72, 81, 89–90
Clemente, Roberto Jr., 64, 95
Clemente, Vera Cristina Zabala, 62, 64, 67, 96
Clendenon, Don, 74
Cleveland Indians, 81
Coates, Jim, 37
Cole, Dick, 37
Colorado Rockies, 95
Concepción, Monchile, 39
Cuellar, Mike, 85, 87

## D

discrimination, 1, 15–17, 57
Dreyfuss, Barney, 67

## E

El Carretero, 70
Ellis, Dock, 83–84
Epsom Derby, 90

## F

Foiles, Hank, 37
Forbes Field, 30, 32, 47, 50, 52, 66–67, 78–79
Ford, Whitey, 50–52, 72
Franks, Herman, 25
Frau, Miguel J., 63

## G

Galbreath, John, 90
García, Arturo, 57, 75
Gehrig, Lou, 51
Gibson, Josh, 11
Gold Glove, 60, 95
Gómez, Rubén, 39
Gonzalez, Juan, 97
Groat, Dick, 48, 50, 53, 58

## H

Haney, Fred, 29–30, 35
Havana Sugar Kings, 20
Hebner, Richie, 86
Hernon, Jack, 32
Hoak, Don, 50, 59
Hornsby, Rogers, 43–44
Houston Astros, 73–74, 82

## I

International League, 17
International Series, 62
Irvin, Monte, 8–9, 96

## J

Jackson, Reggie, 83

## K

Killebrew, Harmon, 83
King, Martin Luther Jr., 73–74
Koufax, Sandy, 9, 69